D0057220

Date Due

DISCARD
THIS ITEM IS NO LONGER
THE PROPERTY OF
MOUNT ROYAL UNIVERSITY

MOUNT ROYAL COLLEGE
LEARNING RESOURCE CENTER

SCRIPPS

SCRIPPS
THE DIVIDED DYNASTY

JACK CASSERLY

DONALD I. FINE, INC.
NEW YORK

Copyright © 1993 by Mr. and Mrs. Edward W. Scripps

All rights reserved, including the right of reproduction in whole or in part in any form. Published in the United States of America by Donald I. Fine, Inc. and in Canada by General Publishing Company Limited.

Library of Congress Catalogue Card Number: 93-70897

ISBN: 1-55611-378-1

Manufactured in the United States of America

10   9   8   7   6   5   4   3   2   1

Designed by Irving Perkins Associates

*For small-town, community newspapermen
and women across America—the grassroots
of our country.*

ACKNOWLEDGMENTS

This book was written with the cooperation of Mr. and Mrs. E.W. Scripps. I spent a month interviewing them—together and separately—at their home and office in Charlottesville, Virginia. They opened some seventy years of personal and professional files to my wife, Joy, and me. These metal drawers cover all four walls of a conference room thirty-seven feet long and eight feet wide. The 172 drawers contain more than 50,000 pages of business memos and correspondence, various news studies, accounting statements, personal letters, newspaper and magazine articles, photos of all types and family memorabilia. Joy spent a month researching the contents. Most of the information in this work came from those files, the Scrippses' interviews, visits to Scripps League newspapers and meetings with executives and staff members, talks with longtime news colleagues outside the Scripps organization, and the E.W. Scripps Papers at Ohio University's Alden Library.

The idea for this undertaking came from Ed and Betty Scripps. I had finished a book (*The Hearsts: Father and Son*) with Bill Hearst and his wife, Austine. The Scrippses were friends of the Hearsts and were thinking of doing a book themselves. Unfortunately Austine, who waged a very courageous battle against bone-marrow cancer, died on June 23, 1991, before she was able to facilitate our meeting.

Austine introduced us to the Scrippses from her grave. She had left that lasting a memory to all of us. The tall, willowy woman with the deep voice would have chuckled and had a quip or two about that. Perhaps she did anyway. I have felt her presence in writing these pages.

Scores of people contributed to this book—from the East Coast to Hawaii. No one offered more help than my wife, Joy, who did most of the research. And no one gave me more good organizational counsel and better editing advice than my longtime friend, James W. Smith, a Phoenix attorney.

I traveled for more than a month to Scripps League newspapers across the nation and to their Herndon, Virginia, administrative-service headquarters. For some 175 hours, I interviewed publishers, editors, reporters, advertising and composing-room staffers. Also readers who critiqued these papers. No one gave me more accurate assistance and guidance than Mark Hinueber, the League's legal counsel. Other Scripps executives and staff who helped were:

Barry Scripps, Roger Warkins, Jack Morgan, Tom Wendel, Keith Curtis, Kirk Parkinson, Earl Biederman, Lloyd Pletsch, Rich Heintz, Greg Stevens, Doug Ernst, Platt Cline, Don Rowley, Mike Patrick, Paul Sweitzer, John Shields, Wayne Agaer, Karen White, John Uyeno, Edith Tanimoto, Bill Haigwood, Karla U. Nedwied, Elaine Maxcy, Lisa Wildman, Doug Zerkel, Shirley Dixon, Ellen Jones, Ray Barber, and others who did not wish to be named in the book.

Former League executives who were interviewed included: Duane Hagadone, Jim Garner, Robert S. Howard, Phil Swift, Phil Buckner and Howard Mendenhall. Others did not wish to be identified.

E.W. Scripps Company chairman Charles Scripps gave us a long interview at the firm's Cincinnati headquarters. Richard Boehne, director of the company's Corporate Communications and Investor Relations, and staffer Greg Hartel also assisted.

Vance H. Trimble, veteran Scripps-Howard newsman and author of *The Astonishing Mr. Scripps* (Iowa State University Press), and his wife, Elzene, graciously received my wife and me at their home in Covington, Kentucky. Trimble answered many questions and offered expert research guidance.

Dr. George Bain, director of the Department of Archives and Special Collections at Ohio University's Alden Library in Athens, assisted me in researching the E.W. Scripps Papers there.

I read various books on the life of E.W. Scripps but frankly found them wanting, except for the Trimble book, which I used to double-check facts and dates. As the reader may note, I took a different approach than Trimble's work. Various library news clippings and articles helped in checking facts as well as filling out many areas of the Scripps family's life and times.

Editor & Publisher was invaluable in checking facts and figures on the U.S. newspaper industry. Don Brod, longtime executive secretary of the International Society of Weekly Newspaper Editors, was a major source of information on small-town newspapers. Brod is a retired journalism professor from Northern Illinois University at De Kalb.

Washington lawyers Lloyd N. Cutler and Robert P. Stranahan, Jr., who have long advised Ed and Betty Scripps on legal matters, covered their responsibilities and reflections well.

It's almost impossible to list all the people and sources who contributed to this book but their assistance is duly noted. My literary agent, Oscar Collier, is last but not least among those whose quiet support helped make this work possible.

All of the above helped prepare for my long question-and-answer sessions with Ed and Betty Scripps.

My gratitude to all who joined in this undertaking. Let us hope that this work may make a genuine contribution to the history of American journalism.

CONTENTS

PREFACE

The Scrippses are in some ways the First Family of American journalism. Their Penny Papers of the last century were the nation's first popular press—low on cost, high on sensationalism and soaring into mass circulation. The Scrippses practiced Yellow Journalism long before William Randolph Hearst and Joseph Pulitzer made it a household phrase. They created the nation's first major chain of newspapers—from their start in Detroit and Cleveland to San Diego and other parts of the West Coast. They were the principal founders of United Press, whose wire service eventually stretched to all parts of the world. And they may well be the most cussed, feuding, fighting lot that ever put out a newspaper.

E.W. Scripps, founder of the empire, was as colorful as any individual in the history of American newspapering. He drank more whiskey, cavorted with more women and smoked more bad cigars than Hearst, Pulitzer and most of their contemporaries put together. Scripps raised more business and family hell than any of the media giants in their wildest moments of rage or elation. He also philosophized and wrote more about newspapers and social issues than almost any American publisher.

Scripps got along with almost nobody. He cut off his beloved

E.W. Scripps in his prime.

eldest son Jim, who had served him well, and cast him adrift. He turned over his empire to his son Robert, who had long been an idler, a drunk and inept. Scripps also made Robert the trustee of his Scripps Trust.

Jim continued in newspapering on his own but died a few years after the break with his father. Jim's wife Josephine, mother of his four children, formally split with Scripps after a bitter lawsuit, launching her own newspaper company, the Scripps League, in 1931. She sued the Scripps Trust for $6 million in salary and other compensation which she claimed E.W. owed her husband. The court case attracted national attention. In the end, the widow believed she had been betrayed by her most trusted confidant—her husband's brother Robert. Josephine's sons, Ed and Jim, took over the firm from their mother but they too fought and split the Scripps League in 1978.

The Scripps dynasty has been divided—and subdivided—for more than sixty years. The E.W. Scripps Company has prospered as a national chain of big dailies. The Scripps League of Newspapers has been since 1950 one of the country's foremost chains of small-town community newspapers. Their philosophy, under Ed and Betty Scripps, is considerably different than that of Scripps-Howard, the newspaper subsidiary of the E.W. Scripps Company. Pioneer Newspapers, the chain formed by Ed's brother Jim after the 1978 split, survives as a small chain but, in typical Scripps fashion, a break occurred. Jim's two daughters inherited Pioneer and one has now bought out the other.

This work, although filled with details of the Scripps family battles, is mostly two other stories: the lives of Ed and Betty Scripps as leaders in community journalism and the contrast between big-city and small-town newspapers. It attempts to show the shades of difference, sometimes night and day, between the so-called Eastern media elite and grassroots newspapers across the rest of the country. Ed Scripps argues that the job of newspapers should be to identify with a community, to serve as a forum for its issues, and be of service to that community. Not to try to set the agenda for that town, the nation or the world.

I've been a reporter most of my forty-three-year career—foreign and domestic—covering stories in forty-eight of the fifty states and some sixty countries around the world. From wars in Korea, the Middle East, Algeria and Vietnam, to the White House and Capitol Hill in Washington, and New York from Broadway to Wall Street. I've finally come home to Prescott, Arizona, a mountain town of about 26,000 people, from where America and the world have another perspective.

This work reflects that distant, more detached view. It is a paean—a hymn of thanksgiving and joy to the gods—in praise and honor of millions of unsung Americans who are the nation's grass-roots. And especially to our fellow citizens manning the citadels of community service on small-town newspapers. It is the song of the wind on the American prairie.

—Jack Casserly
Prescott, Arizona, 1993

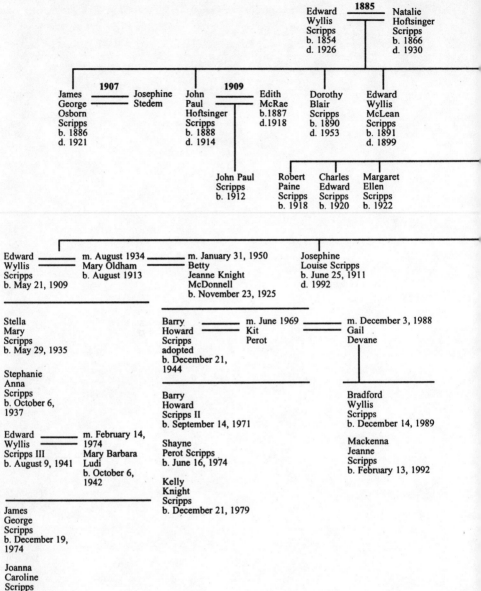

Edward Wyllis Scripps
b. 1854
d. 1926
——— 1885 ———
Natalie Hoftsinger Scripps
b. 1866
d. 1930

James George Osborn Scripps
b. 1886
d. 1921
——— 1907 ———
Josephine Stedem

John Paul Hoftsinger Scripps
b. 1888
d. 1914
——— 1909 ———
Edith McRae
b.1887
d.1918

Dorothy Blair Scripps
b. 1890
d. 1953

Edward Wyllis McLean Scripps
b. 1891
d. 1899

John Paul Scripps
b. 1912

Robert Paine Scripps
b. 1918

Charles Edward Scripps
b. 1920

Margaret Ellen Scripps
b. 1922

Edward Wyllis Scripps
b. May 21, 1909
——— m. August 1934 ———
Mary Oldham
b. August 1913
——— m. January 31, 1950 ———
Betty Jeanne Knight McDonnell
b. November 23, 1925

Josephine Louise Scripps
b. June 25, 1911
d. 1992

Stella Mary Scripps
b. May 29, 1935

Barry Howard Scripps
adopted
b. December 21, 1944
——— m. June 1969 ———
Kit Perot
——— m. December 3, 1988 ———
Gail Devane

Stephanie Anna Scripps
b. October 6, 1937

Barry Howard Scripps II
b. September 14, 1971

Bradford Wyllis Scripps
b. December 14, 1989

Edward Wyllis Scripps III
b. August 9, 1941
——— m. February 14, 1974 ———
Mary Barbara Ludi
b. October 6, 1942

Shayne Perot Scripps
b. June 16, 1974

Mackenna Jeanne Scripps
b. February 13, 1992

Kelly Knight Scripps
b. December 21, 1979

James George Scripps
b. December 19, 1974

Joanna Caroline Scripps
b. December 6, 1976

Descendants of Edward Wyllis Scripps (E.W. Scripps)

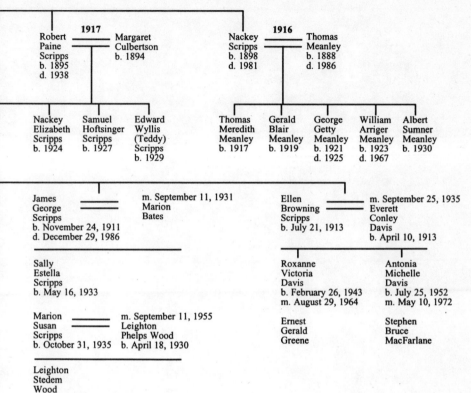

1917
Robert Paine Scripps b. 1895 d. 1938 —— Margaret Culbertson b. 1894

1916
Nackey Scripps b. 1898 d. 1981 —— Thomas Meanley b. 1888 d. 1986

Nackey Elizabeth Scripps b. 1924

Samuel Hoftsinger Scripps b. 1927

Edward Wyllis (Teddy) Scripps b. 1929

Thomas Meredith Meanley b. 1917

Gerald Blair Meanley b. 1919

George Getty Meanley b. 1921 d. 1925

William Arriger Meanley b. 1923 d. 1967

Albert Sumner Meanley b. 1930

James George Scripps b. November 24, 1911 d. December 29, 1986 —— m. September 11, 1931 Marion Bates

Ellen Browning Scripps b. July 21, 1913 —— m. September 25, 1935 Everett Conley Davis b. April 10, 1913

Sally Estella Scripps b. May 16, 1933

Roxanne Victoria Davis b. February 26, 1943 m. August 29, 1964

Antonia Michelle Davis b. July 25, 1952 m. May 10, 1972

Marion Susan Scripps b. October 31, 1935 —— m. September 11, 1955 Leighton Phelps Wood b. April 18, 1930

Ernest Gerald Greene

Stephen Bruce MacFarlane

Leighton Stedem Wood b. June 25, 1956

Compiled by Lavinia V. Walton genealogist Browning, Ill.

GRANDFATHER'S TEN-DOLLAR GOLD PIECE

The sun looked like a great gold coin as it began to set beyond the Blue Ridge Mountains of Virginia. The evening wind blew the May crop of hay in long, slow waves below. Edward Wyllis "Ed" Scripps, Jr., ambled back and forth, cane in hand, on his veranda about a dozen miles outside of Charlottesville. At the age of eighty-four, he had survived his grandfather's coldblooded banishment.

The original Edward Wyllis Scripps, one of the most successful pioneers in American newspaper history, had disinherited Ed's father his eldest son Jim. E.W., as Grandfather Scripps was known, never forgave Jim for leaving the business. Two years after Jim's untimely death, in a bizarre act of vengeance, E.W. rewrote his will, creating the Edward W. Scripps Trust and ensuring that none of Jim's four children would ever share in his multimillion dollar fortune.

E.W. Scripps with his
firstborn grandson,
E.W. Scripps, Jr., at
Miramar in 1909.

Ed pulled down a sea cap to shade his eyes from the bright gold. He enjoyed watching the rolling hills of the Virginia countryside, smelling the hay, and listening to the billowing wind below. It was a quiet comfort for starting on a new road and creating his own news organization from Massachusetts to Hawaii—without so much as a handshake from his grandfather. Yet Ed loved the old man and still does. He had learned so much from E.W.—good and bad.

Ed's thoughts wandered back to his boyhood. He could see and hear E.W., not the rip-roaring rascal some outsiders portrayed, but the great patriarch and philosopher.

As Ed sat in one of the cushioned white wicker chairs on the veranda, he could view much of the 193-acre farm he and his wife Betty call "Eagle Hill."

Ed's mind often wandered back to a faraway time and place—the rolling waves of the Pacific near San Diego where he was born in

1909, and then some seventeen miles north to the old man's vast "Rancho Miramar" (the ranch with a view of the sea). He could picture E.W. standing in the courtyard of his forty-seven-room house there. The big fellow wore a full white scraggly beard, baggy pants and English Wellington-style knee-high boots, a frontiersman's cotton shirt and a billed cap. The cap was pulled down tightly over one eye which sometimes seemed to stray, giving E.W. the appearance of an "evil eye." The old man tramped back and forth, gruffly firing questions at little Eddie. He carried ten-dollar gold coins in his pockets. If the boy gave the right answer to one of E.W.'s science, history or geography questions, he would be rewarded with one of the magnificent gold coins.

Ed, named Junior although he was a grandson, was only five years old when his grandfather began these rounds of scholastic inquiry. Despite his tender age, Ed always knew he was in the presence of power. He had no idea, however, just how much authority and influence his grandfather held in his large frame. In those days, E.W. was one of the country's mightiest newspaper barons.

Nor was the child aware that his grandfather was one of the most colorful individualists in the history of American journalism— indeed, of American life. E.W. had an insatiable hunger for knowledge combined with unconventional ideas of his own. He was an explosive intellectual mixture.

Scripps devoted eighteen years of his life to scholarship. He wrote about 500 "disquisitions"—formal serious discourses. Rather than scholarly judgments, however, the essays were a breathtaking panorama of ideas. These ranged from philosophy and religion to sociology and anthropology. Some of the conclusions were contradictory, such as his editorial support for socialism while extolling entrepreneurial individualism. But the hunger to explore, the fire to understand were always there, brushing aside the contrasts and contradictions, as E.W. plowed the frontiers of his mind.

Scripps saw himself as a champion of the rights and hopes of the average American, yet he wanted little to do with common folk personally. E.W. himself was a commoner, a country bumpkin who had fled the farm.

E.W. Scripps in courtyard at Miramar. The boots were practical: the surrounding foothills were full of rattlesnakes. Circa 1909.

Little Eddie knew that grandfather was not only master of Miramar, but of all the adults and children who lived there at his invitation. Eddie was also sure that some lucky day he would win some of the gold coins that grandfather carried in his pockets.

In this recollected summer at the start of World War I, E.W. was sixty years old. He was born in 1854 in the small farm town of Rushville, Illinois, the thirteenth child of his father's three marriages. E.W. was eventually termed by others, and admitted by himself, to be "a damned old crank." The monicker, as he referred to the portrayal, followed the patriarch to his grave. However, the description was not the only sobriquet used by enemies, family and friends. He was also called an eccentric, a radical, scoundrel, an argumentative troublemaker, a still rising entrepreneur, miser, patron of the underdog, home-grown philosopher, hermit, visionary and genius. And some epithets too strong for his newspapers and the public stomach. Only the brash William Randolph Hearst rivaled E.W. in this wide swath of character contradiction.

To Eddie the towering figure of his grandfather projected not only power but an aura of greatness. He was mesmerized by his grandfather's commanding presence, deep-throated voice (some said E.W. bellowed like a hog-caller), high boots, and gold coins.

Grandfather preferred boots for tramping through the high grass and scratchy desert brush to avoid the rattlesnakes which roamed the Southern California foothills. He would stomp a bothersome snake to death without breaking stride, and sometimes unwind a swift kick at menacing coyotes. The boots also allowed him to escape loose dirt and pebbles that often annoyed those in low shoes. Eddie was amazed that E.W. took off his boots so easily. Such ease in the face of so great a challenge made grandfather an even larger figure.

But it was the gold coins that lit up Eddie's eyes. Grandfather would shift them one at a time as he paced the length of the inner courtyard of the ranch house. The master was measuring the distance of his daily exercise while questioning Eddie, his brother Jim, and later their sisters Ellen and Josephine. E.W.'s other grandchildren also joined in the competition. These question sessions were terribly exciting. The mere thought of winning a ten-dollar gold coin caused Eddie's head to spin. In those days, that was a half-month's pay for some ranch hands.

As soon as his grandchildren could read, E.W. began giving them books—about Alaska, Siberia, North Africa, the Middle East. Science, economics, government, history, philosophy. The old man glamorized reading and learning. He implied that serious study was more fun than flying kites. However, the grandchildren clearly preferred hoisting their homemade contraptions on trips into the wild blue skies.

Many of the gift books were far above the youngsters' ages and heads. But if one were to be blessed by a gold coin from grandfather, he must read. They also wanted to please the old man because he was nice to them. He did not stomp around in fury, as they heard from some complainers in the compound. Indeed not. He spoke of education with reverence. School was here, all around Miramar. He was a teacher and so were the tutors he hired for them. They need not go to San Diego with about 25,000 people suffocating in a crowded city, where the schoolhouses were often filled with pests, human and animal. No, the old man told them solemnly, they could learn at Miramar and build their bodies and brains in the fresh country air.

Despite the difficulty of E.W.'s many questions, Eddie, his brother and sisters, and their cousins finally astounded their patriarch and started coming up with some right answers on Siberia, science, or some faraway subject. Eddie never forgot the day he won his first gold piece. It was a question about Alaska. The gold shone brilliantly because grandfather had been rubbing the coin in his pockets for days and perhaps weeks. It wasn't mere money to Eddie. It was symbolic of achievement, a sign recognized in every country and backwater town in the world. The passport to earth's Shining City. For a five-year-old boy, it was his first triumph in life.

Ed recalls Miramar and his grandfather with affection. Other descendents and business associates of old E.W. have criticized and some even cursed him. The old man feuded bitterly for twenty-four years with his own older brother James, who gave E.W. his start in newspapering. He later fought with his eldest son Jim and cut off Jim's widow Josephine and her four children from their inheritance from his estate. That included little Eddie, who loved him. This family-shattering blow by a man who saw himself as a philosopher was perhaps the most unreasonable act of his long and stormy life. It caused a division of the Scripps media dynasty that endures to this day—seventy years later.

Now, the aging man on the Virginia veranda, the eldest of the youngsters whom his grandfather inexplicably shunned, has fashioned his own legacy. Ed has created a new direction and vision in the Scripps legend with no help from his grandfather. He has built his own chain of newspapers across small-town America. Ed has embraced the common man and the country's grassroots—communities from New England to the Hawaiian island of Kauai.

E.W.'s quarrels with other members of the family persisted after the split with son Jim and daughter-in-law Josephine. He battled with his son Robert and nearly gave up on the young man. Bob, as he was known among family and friends, had fallen in love with Helen McRae, daughter of one of E.W.'s longtime business partners. The old man believed the young lady to be a wily siren luring his son into her bed and, hopefully, a wealthy marriage. He rebuffed Bob as immature for his dabbling in poetry and lack of marketable professional skills. Bob was not a fighter. He eventually succumbed to his father's admonishments and embraced virtually everything the old man dictated. Bob and his descendents were thus bequeathed virtually all of E.W.'s legacy. This is represented today by the large and powerful E.W. Scripps Company, a media conglomerate, better known as Scripps-Howard.

E.W. clashed with his daughter Nackey in 1916 because she eloped with his secretary, Tom Meanley. The old man never accepted Meanley as part of the family. Indeed, Scripps treated him as a dead man. Finally, E.W. collided continuously with his wife Nackie, causing the two to live virtually separate lives in their later years.

Of the patriarch's six children, only two didn't become embroiled with their father—Edward Wyllis McLean, the youngest son who died at the age of five, and Dorothy, called "Dolla," who was mentally crippled by a birth injury.

E.W.'s splintered personality emerged more clearly as his life progressed. His public portrait was less that of a man and more one of a human enigma. He was at the same time a common drunk and an omnivorous reader; a woman chaser and a self-educated philosopher. A multimillionaire and one who understood profoundly that money does not make the man. A recluse and an individual who sought to influence not only the American masses but the president and other leading figures of the United States.

Understanding E.W. was to comprehend something of the

mighty American individualists—the Morgans, Vanderbilts, Fords, Harrimans, Hartfords and Hearsts—of his time. What have he and they wrought? What in their explosive lives defines them?

For Ed Scripps, all the questions and answers began with E.W.'s father, James Mogg Scripps. He had been a London bookbinder who had gone bankrupt twice. Both of his wives had died, leaving him with six surviving children. James's father then visited two brothers who had settled in Rushville, Illinois, and purchased 160 acres within walking distance of the Rushville courthouse, intending to start anew. En route to the farm town, James stopped in Ohio to visit family friends, the Osborns. He met and later married Julia Adeline Osborn, the schoolteacher daughter, with whom he would have five more children. The last was named Edward Wyllis, or E.W.

As a boy, he gathered kindling, drove the family cows, chopped wood, and worked in the fields. However, as E.W. grew older, the young man got others to do much of his work. That allowed him to spend more time reading in the large family library, much of which had come from London. Young E.W. was not about to remain down on the farm.

He became aware early that his family had been learned book people—in literary London no less. Other relatives owned Rushville weekly newspapers. A cousin had helped found the Chicago *Tribune* and Chicago *Democratic Press*. The Scrippses were somebodies.

Yet, young Eddie sometimes felt unwanted by his mother, and felt closest to his sister Ellen, eighteen years older, Ellen, short and homespun, was closer to him than his mother. She was sweet, serene, and the only family member to graduate from college. The two formed an unbreakable bond that was to last throughout their lives. At school, he was often left out of games and taunted because rheumatic knees caused him to stumble. The youngster withdrew from his schoolmates and would, as he later admitted, suffer a lifetime of loneliness. He dropped out of school at fifteen because his aging father needed him to work on the farm. He was happy to leave his taunters. His sister Ellen had been teaching him at home since the age of three.

Eddie managed to make money on wood sawing and other labor by organizing outside help. He had a sure eye for work shortcuts and slashing labor costs. He effectively became the farm boss. His father, Ellen and others in the family soon realized that, with his quick, innovative mind, Eddie should leave the farm for some large city and greater financial rewards in business or industry.

At the age of eighteen, E.W. put on his first store-bought suit, hopped a train and headed for Detroit. He was already an imposing figure with massive shoulders, a bull neck and big head. His half brothers James and George took the young farmer on as a part-time office boy at their newspaper, the Detroit *Tribune*. James believed that Ellen had spoiled E.W. rotten and wanted the young upstart to prove himself at someone else's expense, so he got E.W. a job with relatives as an apprentice at a nearby pharmacy.

The newcomer distinguished himself at neither the paper nor the pharmacy but by forming a manufacturing partnership and selling window blinds. Then the *Tribune* burned down, less than six months after E.W.'s arrival. It was a heaven-sent blaze!

The Scrippses received what they considered an astonishing $30,000 in insurance money. They could start a better paper with newer equipment and more work space. James and George launched the Detroit *Evening News*. That was the beginning of the Scripps empire. Its news editing and writing were founded on a simple formula which James adapted from *The Peter Parley Tales*. The small book, brought from England by their father, contained short stories about romance, crime and travel. The news format was starkly basic: condense stories into simple language that even a child would understand. The format for quick, easy reading would literally sweep across American newspapers like a prairie fire.

James became an innovator in newspaper size by printing a smaller-size six-column, four-page daily. It sold at only two cents a copy on the street and ten cents for six days of home delivery. The Scrippses also were pioneers in out-of-town home delivery.

E.W. was later to adapt and improve on the Peter Parley formula: championing the masses and accenting human, reader-interest stories. Underselling the competition by keeping costs low. He hired bright executives, shunning bank loans if at all possible, and holding company stock closely.

The Scrippses added three newspapers to the *News* in these early years—the Cleveland *Press,* Cincinnati *Post,* and St. Louis *Chronicle*—and formed the country's first major newspaper chain. However, James and E.W. were constantly feuding—from quarreling about how and when to spend money to who was in charge of editorial policy. Another point of contention was E.W.'s social swashbuckling. He launched into a whirl of wenching and claimed to drink a gallon of whiskey a day. He later lowered that estimate, perhaps even his drinking, to a quart.

E.W.'s hands began to shake and his mind became soggy from whiskey. He tried to escape his peccadilloes by touring Europe. E.W. later sailed to North Africa and other faraway shores. Scripps loved the sea and was to spend many of his final years on oceans far from his wife and family.

His drinking bouts ultimately won the newsman the unsalubrious label of being an alcoholic. Everyone in the Scripps family was aware that E.W. was a two-fisted tippler but some of his big boozing and eccentric behavior startled even them.

Scripps once flatly turned down an invitation to lunch with President Woodrow Wilson. Wilson invited E.W. to the White House when the news chief visited Washington in 1914. Scripps had been on the road for more than two months and missed the peace of his Miramar hideaway. E.W.'s head and stomach ached from whiskey and cigars. He was also carrying a load of business problems. So when the White House called him at his hotel, Scripps growled that he was in no mood to have lunch with anyone that day and hung up.

.E.W. had been telling friends and associates that Wilson acted too much like a college professor, the president's earlier occupation, and not enough like a leader. As anyone who was acquainted with E.W. knew, Scripps didn't think that college professors knew how to put on their socks. E.W.'s criticism of Wilson's leadership drifted back to the president, who apparently was determined to win the newsman's respect and support.

Slowly and grudgingly, Scripps realized that he had made a

E.W. Scripps, Jr., at age 2.

colossal blunder in rejecting the presidential luncheon. Friends and the White House staff finally intervened and E.W. saw Wilson. The two hit it off well after each conceded that the other was a man of intellect and goodwill.

In drinking, grandson Ed explains, the old man saw himself as a "macho guy" who followed the tradition of the times. In those days, a man's man drank, sometimes by the bucket, and E.W. swallowed barrels of the stuff. But he managed to quit for long periods and could become intolerant of men who allowed booze to interfere with their professional performance.

All of E.W.'s sons drank and some suggested alcoholism might run in the family.

E.W.'s battles rumbled much beyond his family. Not long after becoming publisher of the Cleveland *Press* at the age of twenty-four, he was sued for libel. The *Press* was known as a Penny Paper because it was sold at a cheaper price than others. A wealthy Cleveland steel-company owner and socialite, Henry Chisholm, claimed he was maligned. The *Press* alleged that one of the tycoon's sons beat up a prostitute in public. Chisholm's workers nabbed the reporter when he visited the steel chief's office to explain that he had confused Chisholm's son with his brother. The steel workers painted the newsman black from head to foot and, to cap the episode off, dumped a bucket of black paint over his head as Chisholm watched. The tycoon also hired thugs and roused mobs against Scripps. E.W. flailed back at him in his paper. Charges and counterclaims titil-lated Cleveland society for weeks. Chisholm was embarrassed and finally surrendered by withdrawing the libel suit and paying the reporter a handsome indemnity. Scripps had little remorse about the incident.

E.W.'s tempestuous love life was not much different. Various women popped in and out of his life like one-act plays but one angry mistress went public. Elizabeth Brown not only confronted E.W. at his desk in the Cleveland *Press* but told other newspapers that her onetime lover was a two-bit, no-good, lying rascal. Her four-alarm fire was eventually put out but not before Scripps had been taught a lesson—be good to bad girls.

E.W. smoked his way through more cigars than most railroad roughnecks or mining men did in a lifetime. He quit smoking more times than a born-again Christian denounced sin. As a result of all the booze and cigars—and coughing—Scripps fantasized the worst: that he had developed tuberculosis and cancer. Neither proved true but they helped keep his physicians in financial good health for much of his life. So too did his lifelong complaints of shattered nerves and other forms of hypochondria.

After all his hell-raising, E.W. fell in love with a parson's daughter. The tough newspaper chief thought he was in heaven when he met Nackie Holtsinger. The chance encounter came at, of all places, a church social in West Chester, Ohio, in May of 1885. Scripps had been talked into going to the affair by a friend. Nackie was nine-teen, twelve years his junior, and he first regarded her as only a "very beautiful child." Nackie had, however, graduated from high school and had a poise far beyond her years. She played the organ, sang in the church choir, and planned to teach music. Scripps was smitten with her. It was a whirlwind four-month courtship.

If there was a period in his life when Scripps was truly happy, it was the early years of his marriage to Nackie. Her father no sooner conducted the Presbyterian service than the couple rushed to the train for a honeymoon in West Virginia and Virginia. On the month-long holiday, the young bride also saw the Atlantic Ocean, Chesapeake Bay and Washington, D.C., for the first time. When Nackie arrived home in Cincinnati by train, the newlywed discovered that she was already expecting her first child. She would not disappoint her pleased husband. It would be a boy, James George Scripps. She was to bear him five more children.

After marrying, E.W. began easing his brother James out of power by establishing a working partnership with brother George and Milton McRae, his chief of staff. They formed a new organization and named it the Scripps-McRae League. E.W. assumed power as trustee of his partners' holdings. James, who had been ill, retained stock in the company but seemed relieved that his brother took over actual leadership of the organization. He died in 1904. A generation of feuding between the brothers had mercifully ended but the fight was a forerunner of the family's continuous conflicts.

By 1906, in bursts of enthusiasm, E.W. and McRae expanded the league to twenty newspapers. They were unique because Scripps, while owning at least fifty-one percent of each paper, allowed his executives to buy stock in the publications. He also allowed his editors a free rein in running them.

Scripps and McRae, who worked together for more than twenty-five years, were at odds much of that time. Other executives also clashed with Scripps. E.W.'s internal business squabbles seemed interminable.

Scripps and McRae later collided over the marriage of one of E.W.'s sons, John Paul, to McRae's daughter, Edith. The old man was wary of the McRae girls because he felt that Edith's sister Helen had

earlier attempted to trap his son Bob into marriage. He also sus-
pected McRae himself of quietly promoting both romances to enhance his own power within the company. E.W. didn't attend the
wedding but few were shocked. He often sidestepped important
family occasions.

The Scripps-McRae relationship nose-dived over their mutual
grandson, John Paul, Jr. McRae applied for guardianship of the
five-year-old after John Paul's early passing and while Edith lay on
her deathbed. Scripps wanted the youngster to live with him at
Miramar. McRae violently objected and eventually became the boy's
guardian.

In the same way that the two had gotten rid of James, E.W. then
coolly disbanded the Scripps-McRae League and formed the
Scripps-Howard organization. McRae retired. Brash, flamboyant
Roy Howard, described by some as a boy genius, had come to E.W.'s
attention as the chief of his United Press wire service. The old man
decided, after much soul-searching, that Howard was as good a
choice as any for executive editor to help run his papers. It was said
E.W. acted against McRae out of personal spite but he and his longtime aide later healed the wound. The incident was nevertheless
significant because E.W.'s callousness was a forerunner of his coldblooded heartlessness toward his son Jim and Jim's wife Josephine.
Later, under McRae's tutelage, John Paul, Jr., formed his own newspaper chain. Ironically, it merged in 1987 with Scripps-Howard.

Bob Scripps took the reins of the new organization with Roy
Howard. Roy and E.W. soon clashed over this dual leadership. Roy
demanded that he alone run the organization. He viewed Bob as
inexperienced and weak. In a lengthy ultimatum to E.W., Roy
threatened to resign if he didn't become top man. The bow-tied
little rooster finally quit crowing and returned to work when
Scripps wouldn't budge.

E.W., an untrained country clodhopper who educated himself
with the help of his sister Ellen, eventually owned or controlled
forty-one newspapers. Nine died or were folded. Others were added
after E.W. passed control of the organization to Bob. These papers
ranged from early publications like the Detroit *News*, Cleveland

Press and Cincinnati *Post* to papers in such cities as New York, Chicago, Kansas City, Des Moines, Akron, Denver, Dallas, Houston, Los Angeles, San Francisco and Seattle. One of Scripps's greatest battles occurred in St. Louis where he challenged Joseph Pulitzer and, surprising only himself, lost. But it was only a skirmish. Scripps was to win the American newspaper war.

E.W. not only built America's first major newspaper chain but created the United Press wire service, perhaps his greatest journalistic achievement. He also launched the Newspaper Enterprise Association, a news-feature, illustrations, and comics syndicate that has long spanned the globe.

Scripps owned mostly afternoon newspapers but he felt the Associated Press daily wire service report favored morning papers. Top breaking news was often held back for Eastern morning papers since the AP was organized by New York dailies. The AP, composed of member papers, emerged after the Civil War to help Eastern papers escape the cost of heavy telegraph tolls. E.W. also was upset because the wire service granted exclusive publication rights to clients in their circulation areas. Scripps would thus be at a disadvantage when he wanted to start a rival paper in many towns. E.W. and other publishers were concerned about AP creating a monopoly.

In response, Chicago newspapers launched a second wire service. Shortly before the turn of this century, however, the agency went bankrupt. Scripps, by obtaining the support of papers across the country, resurrected it and helped make it a global news-gathering organization. The financial undertaking was enormous and proved E.W. had real guts. He named it the Scripps-McRae Press Association, which later became United Press. It became United Press International (UPI) when the service merged with Hearst's International News Service (INS) in 1958. The UP not only competed with AP, INS and foreign news agencies, but beat them on countless major stories across the world.

Over the past decade, UPI has had several owners and bordered on bankruptcy despite its rich, colorful history. The wire service was finally rescued from drowning in 1992 when the Middle East

Broadcasting Center (MBC) purchased it for about four million dollars. London-based MBC is owned primarily by Saudi Arabian businessmen. One can only guess what E.W. would have said about this, but he enjoyed his voyages to the Mideast and probably would have grunted: Full speed ahead!

Scripps imbued his papers with a social conscience. He dedicated them to the common man's battle for economic and social justice. He maintained that the "soul" of his papers—community service— would always be placed above profit. Protest became the heartbeat of his publications. As E.W. succinctly put it:

"God damn the rich and God help the poor."

Amid his many conflicts, E.W. first viewed San Diego from a steamship in December of 1890. He was thirty-six years old, and well on the road to national prominence. The temperature was nearly sixty degrees, a pleasant relief from the harsh winters of Cincinnati, Cleveland, and indeed his Rushville birthplace.

E.W. saw the area not only as a winter retreat but as a possible permanent home and working headquarters. He toured the desolate countryside north of San Diego and was reported to have paid an inflated $5,000 for his original 400 acres of land. A later account placed the total at nearly $2,200. Actually, Ed Scripps says, his grandfather paid less than $800 for that first spread. Ed explained the conflicting accounts to make a point: many incidents in E.W.'s life have been reported inaccurately or exaggerated. This is true in some of the books that have been written about him, especially *Lusty Scripps* (Vanguard Press, New York) by Gilson Gardner, longtime Washington correspondent for the Scripps newspapers. That is not to suggest that Scripps was any less of a mind-boggling national figure. He was all of that.

A year after E.W. had bought his first acreage, he and family members boarded a special railroad car and returned West. They lived in the first wing constructed at Miramar. Scripps continued adding to the house and grounds for the next eight years. Four wings surrounded the rectangular, open-ended courtyard. A large fountain stood at the center of the yard. The patio covered three-quarters of an acre. Large windows looked out on bougainvillea

An aerial view of Miramar Ranch in the late 1930s. It covered 2,100 acres and included a 47-room main house and a 32-room bunkhouse for servants.

vines, great forests of graceful eucalyptus trees, cactus gardens and tall, swaying pines. E.W. added a gym and an aviary close to the house. His workers also planted citrus groves, Torrey pines, exotic cacti, and other vegetation. He hired some of his brothers and cousins to oversee the growing "mirage" in the desert.

The ranch house grounds had blossomed to 2,100 acres. E.W. and Nackie lived in a suite of rooms, including an expansive bedroom and large bathroom which also had a massage table and dentist's chair for the dentist who came out from the city when E.W. re quested. The suite included a study and secretary's office. The patriarch didn't go into town except to catch a train East on business, take to the ocean in his yacht, or play cards with a few old cronies at a private club.

Scripps also built guest suites for his executives who came for business meetings. Family and relatives built a dozen homes circling the ranch house. Miramar became Scripps's residence and office, although E.W. continued to claim Ohio as his official residence as a means of completely controlling his estate. E.W.'s residence became a controversial factor in the division of the Scripps dynasty.

Grandmother Nackie sometimes organized dances on the Mexican-tiled outdoor patio of the main house. She put borax chips on the tiles to make them smoother so dancers would have greater freedom of movement. Ed soon gave up dancing because he was too tall and gangly. However, he and other cousins used to enjoy roller skating on the hard maple floors inside the house.

Scripps also constructed a thirty-two-room bunkhouse for servants and other workers—ranch and farm hands, tutors, chauffeurs, cooks and maids. Depending on the season, as many as 100 people worked there. E.W. had also acquired neighboring acreage, calling it Fanita Ranch, and thus owned nearly 10,000 acres. At Fanita, the old man planted great alfalfa fields, lemon trees, and stabled more than fifty brood mares and a prized stallion.

More than two dozen buildings ranged the property as well as electric generators, cisterns, and water reservoirs. E.W. even built more than 100 miles of nearby roads and highways with his own funds. However, he wouldn't repair them, insisting that that was the job of local government. The Scripps family's large local land holdings and precious water rights were later to cause conflict with some residents who felt threatened by their growing presence and power. E.W. frowned on land speculation but some of his family, including his sister Ellen, made large profits from early purchases of large acreage.

Shortly after moving to his oasis, E.W. and two reporters bought the San Diego *Sun*. (In the 1930s, the *Sun* was sold and folded into the San Diego *Tribune*. The *Trib* recently merged with the *Union*.) The *Sun* was the first signal that the Scripps name was to light up the city and much of Southern California.

Ed and other youngsters in the family viewed their grandfather as a humble man of simple desires. They were confused when newspaper reporters and others referred to the large ranch house as a "castle." These writers traced the ranch house's architecture to Emperor Maximilian's Chapultepec castle in Mexico City. The Chapultepec edifice was said to have been copied from Maximilian's "dream house" at Trieste on the Adriatic Sea. The "castle" characterization has been repeated to this day in most documented accounts of Miramar. Yet, as Ed now recalls, neither his grandfather nor any member of the family ever called it that. They knew of no originals in Mexico or Europe. Their only conception of the construction was a Southwestern-style single-story adobe house.

Although E.W. never compared Miramar to the grandiose mansions of William Randolph Hearst at San Simeon, Scripps completed his large undertaking thirty years before Hearst began his "magnificent obsession." The state of California and others now refer to the Hearst complex as the Hearst Castle. Like E.W., Hearst detested what he considered extravagant language. And, in like manner, Hearst called his place "the ranch."

Scripps dug his life deeper and deeper into Miramar. In 1908, E.W. announced that he was "retiring" to his hideaway. Despite this statement, he was as involved in his newspapers as ever. In some respects, however, Scripps became a different man. As lord of the manor, he began sleeping until nearly noon each day. The old man rarely ventured away from Miramar except to go to sea on one of his yachts. Most of all, he happily welcomed the first of his grandchildren, Ed.

One of Ed's lasting memories of his grandfather was the Sunday family meal at Miramar. As many as seventeen or eighteen family members might gather there, with E.W. at the head of the table. The grandchildren were relegated to the foot of the table so they wouldn't interfere with the grownups. They were under orders not to speak. A plate of food and drink was passed to each and heaven help anyone if he spilled anything. Some went to sleep and never ate. Others bawled and had to be picked up. In this way, they got to see what the grownups were eating from the table. Nevertheless, Eddie was content down under so long as the food kept coming and there was hope of dessert.

Ed remembers that E.W. constantly tried to impress his entrepreneurial spirit on the youngsters. Of course, they were too young to comprehend much of what he meant. But they understood the general idea of making money—thus the ability to buy candy, dogs, horses, bicycles and cars—with your own brains and initiative.

Eddie's biggest moments were taking his dog, Nero, and riding his horse, Sinbad, to the far reaches of the foothills. Nero was a large, lumbering Saint Bernard. Wherever the youngster went, Nero was sure to follow, even on long expeditions into the brush with Sinbad. Ed keeps dogs to this day. He now has a Labrador, Cocoa Bear, who also seems to follow him everywhere.

Not all was idyllic at the ranch. Ed recalls knife and icepick fights among some of the Oriental cooks in the kitchen. Ranch hands would get drunk and holler up a storm in the bunkhouse. Some of the drivers, who came from France, loved the San Diego nightlife and often honked their way into the compound at dawn. Many of them carried risque photos of naughty girls which they passed around to anyone with an eye for nudes.

Eddie and his cousins were not spared hard work. At the age of eight, he was already repairing pipelines between water reservoirs. The growing grandson was good with his hands. E.W. furnished Eddie with an extensive tool set and ordered a load of lumber dumped outside the youngster's home. He told his grandson to do something—anything. Eddie built a thirty-five-foot bridge over a gulch to a reservoir which served him and his cousins as a swimming pool. Other projects followed. The grandfather also encouraged Eddie in bicycle, car and other mechanics. The grandson got his first car at the age of ten, a four-wheel cart with a small engine. No equipment was allowed to run down. E.W. encouraged the use of heavy grease. All this constituted what the patriarch called "education."

Ed recalls that he and his grandfather had long walks and warm talks. E.W. could be quite gregarious as he ambled along with a bamboo pole as a cane. They shared a liking for science, mathematics, history and geography. The old man gave Ed a telescope to study the sky and space. E.W. encouraged his grandson to be an original, independent thinker. This meant not only forming his own thoughts and ideas but choosing what was right for him as an individual. The patriarch maintained that self-education, not school, should be an individual's intellectual foundation. Scripps indicated to his grandchildren that he didn't trust public schools from A to Z.

Years earlier, however, the old man had bent that belief. He sent two of his own sons, Jim and John Paul, to the nearby Linda Vista grade school for several years and later to the Harvard School in Los Angeles. He bound his sons closer to home and the land during their summer months. Each was made ranch manager—handling money, hiring and firing workers and straightening out the many daily problems. The idea was to teach them the meaning of work, self-reliance and to draw out their leadership qualities. E.W. was creating foundations for the entrepreneurial spirit.

To emphasize personal responsibility, E.W. called Jim, ten, and John Paul, eight, into his office at Miramar to sign a "contract." Bob was too young. The agreements were typewritten in legalese, and formally bound. They required the sons to pay for all their clothing, toys, and not accept gifts from anyone without the knowledge of E.W. or Nackie. They also were to pay for damages to all property. Finally, they were to tell E.W. if they disobeyed any of his orders or rules.

Ed's family left Miramar during the latter part of World War I for Cincinnati, where his father Jim was assigned to run the organization's headquarters. The Scripps-McRae League was now well established as the first and foremost newspaper chain in the country. Ed's mother Josephine, a devoutly religious woman, placed him in a Christian school. The family returned to Miramar after a stint of about a year and a half.

At the age of ten, Ed, his brother and sisters were enrolled in San Diego's Francis Parker School. The institution was founded by Mrs. Templeton Johnson, a wealthy local woman. She aimed to leave an intellectual impact on the city by attracting the area's brightest

children and drilling them hard. These young elite students were to
be trained for leadership. Brains, not money, was the key to en-
trance. The poor, as well as the middle class and rich, attended. Mrs.
Johnson financed those who couldn't afford the tuition.

The Scripps children invited classmates out to Miramar and it
provoked an uproar among some parents. The Miramar clan soon
became known as a "wild bunch" because the ranch was a three-ring
circus—featuring riding, swimming, hiking, cycling, cow-pie tossing, motorcycle races, and catching rattlesnakes.

Some parents forbade their children to visit Miramar after they
learned that the Scripps children launched sun-baked cow pies at
each other like modern frisbees and snatched the throats of rattlers
with wired sticks.

The Scripps kids caught many rattlers after San Diego officials
announced that snake venom was needed as an antidote to a sharp
increase in poisonous bites. They and some pals were transporting
the snakes in a station wagon to San Diego as part of the serum
campaign. The rattlers were supposed to be imprisoned inside big
gunnysacks but suddenly one of the youngsters discovered that all
the snakes were loose in the rear of the vehicle. Chaos erupted.
They pulled the station wagon to the side of the coastal road and
opened the rear door. Many of the snakes slipped out and were soon
crawling and spitting defiance on the road. Passers-by, some of
whom had never seen a live snake, were horror-stricken. Screaming
women picked up their children and ran. Cars and trucks bolted to
the other side of the road. Those wild Scripps kids were shaking up
the neighborhood again. Fortunately, they recaptured all the snakes
and their serum served the community well.

In the summer months, decades before the arrival of air condi-
tioning, the torrid desert heat at Miramar was almost unbearable. It
sometimes soared over 120 degrees. From early June until the beginning of September, all the grandchildren were taken to E.W.'s
beach house at nearby Del Mar. Much to the youngsters' chagrin,
their tutors went along and they had to read and study most morning hours.

One fall, when the children returned to Miramar from the beach,

E.W. began inviting Ed and other grandchildren to his business meetings. These conferences became part of their education. Sometimes as many as forty executives would gather to discuss the company's problems. The youngsters were to remain silent. No questions or comments were permitted during the conferences. After the meetings the youths were free to ask questions of E.W. or any of his colleagues. The patriarch was running a leadership school although he never termed it that. He was training his successors to run the company with what he called "soul."

At the age of twelve, Ed began driving his brother and sisters about seventeen miles to school in San Diego. They put him behind the wheel of an old Hudson for two reasons: Ed was big enough to crank and start the car, and he could see through the windshield without a cushion. Ed wore farmers' bib overalls to school because he never knew when he might get dirty cranking or fixing the Hudson.

California had no drivers' licenses in those days and, in fact, not many good roads around San Diego. Ed knew a lot about cars because he studied the mechanics of his father's Stanley Steamer. The youngster was fascinated by the car because it was run by steam pressure. His father fired up the Steamer by using a long bamboo pole on which he dipped a bottle of cotton waste. He would ignite the waste and hold it over the car's burner. An explosion would erupt, and the car's hood would fly up. That was the signal for Ed to jump into his seat for the ride.

Ed was soon ready for his own vehicle. His parents bought him a thirty-horsepower motorcycle. He took the cycle apart piece by piece but couldn't put it back together. Embarrassed, he dropped all the pieces into a sack and carted them to a motorcycle repair shop where they put him back on the road.

E.W. often took Ed and his cousins to visit local scientists whom he funded. Some of them later became part of the Scripps Institute of Oceanography and a biological-medical research group which the old man also underwrote. They roared down to La Jolla and nearby towns in grandfather's big Pierce-Arrow. Ed felt like they were driving a tank. Ed remembers meetings with experts on marine biology. One scientist discussed genetic waves. The youngster didn't understand a word of what the man said. On the drive home, E.W. explained that it could all be understood in terms of gurgling water caused by a stuck toilet valve. Ed burst out laughing at his grandfather's explanation. E.W. later wrote a disquisition about genetic waves and toilet valves.

On the road home from many of these auto trips, Scripps often smoked big cigars. Instead of feeling like a conquering general in the Pierce-Arrow, Ed often rolled himself into a ball and surrendered to a stomach ache.

E.W. owned many cars, including Cadillacs and Packards. Half of the auto fleet seemed to be in constant disrepair. The old man did a lot of bellowing about this but knew it was a price he had to pay for the family's life in the isolated countryside.

Ed was happy to return to his motorcycle. He loved the freedom and space of the open road and rode a long string of his own cycles for seventy years. Ed quit at the age of eighty-one because his wife feared he might break his neck. If he could, however, Scripps would ride again tomorrow. He still maintains two motorcycles at Eagle Hill and muses that he may yet sneak away to joyride.

If Ed liked motorcycles, E.W. loved yachts. When Ed was fourteen years old, the old man invited him and some of his schoolmates to take a trip to Ensenada, Mexico, on his new 172-foot yacht, *Ohio*.

When they had crossed from San Diego into Mexican waters, E.W. suggested some "target practice." The youngsters were mystified until the old man explained that the cannon on the foredeck actually fired. So did two machine guns mounted there. The crew floated targets in the ocean when the yacht was about ten nautical miles from the shoreline. Under the guidance of E.W. and the crew, the boys fired salvo after salvo and one gunburst after another. The youngsters didn't hit much but E.W. became an instant hero. Some parents saw him as the wacky elder of the Scripps "wild bunch."

The Scrippses demonstrated every Sunday morning, at least to themselves, that they were not the unholy barbarians that some people thought they were. Ed's mother Josephine began Sunday Bible study. The children of all families and many parents attended. These sessions were to have a profound effect on young Ed.

The Christian faith became one of the most important forces in his life.

E.W. never attended. Some of those who knew him claimed he was an atheist. Others suggested he might be an agnostic. The patriarch brushed off these observations with a wisecrack: I quit going to church because they wouldn't let me smoke a cigar there.

Ed never believed his grandfather to be an atheist. E.W. often read the Bible and quoted from it on numerous occasions. Ed recalls the strongest admonition that the old man ever gave him: Obey the Ten Commandments! However, he also admonished his grand-children: Make money!

E.W. had few close friends. They were, at most, four—his wife Nackie, and sisters Ellen, Annie and Virginia. However, he spent much of his time fighting with Nackie.

Ed remembers his grandmother as a God-fearing, caring woman. She was the first in the family, apart from his own mother Josephine, who was a nurse, to help anyone who was ill. She closely watched weaker members of the family, such as daughter Dorothy, called Dolla, who was mentally retarded. Nackie and E.W. investigated every medical lead they could find to clear Dolla's clouded mind. As a young woman, she had the mental growth of a ten-year-old. Nackie built Dolla her own home with a nurse, servants and a driver. And when he died, E.W. left her a special trust fund.

Scripps was often moody and Nackie had a difficult time coping with his mercurial disposition. Yet she cared deeply for E.W. and became lonely when he was away on a trip.

Nackie was alarmed at times by self-perceived health problems and became almost hysterical with worry about her aches. This anxiety crept into her relations with others, particularly E.W. Nackie also could still be jealous. She was outraged when her husband hired an American nurse in China to accompany him on voyages abroad. There was never an affair but Nackie was so upset that she suggested the mere presence of the woman might be grounds for divorce. In his final years, E.W.'s relationship with Nackie became so painful that his doctors suggested he take long vacations from his wife. He did.

Ellen Browning
Scripps, E.W.'s older
sister, at age 92. She
understood E.W. bet-
ter than anyone.

Ed recalls Nackie as fiercely loyal to E.W. despite the tension
between them. Ed cannot remember when his grandmother didn't
want to be with her husband, although, at times, she had difficulty
in cooling her anger over some incident—real or imagined. Ed
finally measured the relationship in his own words: "You can love
someone but he or she can still irritate the hell out of you."

Scripps's sister Ellen, who never married, was not only the closest
to him of his brothers and sisters but understood E.W. better than
anyone. Their identities were so close that some people dealt with
the two like mother and son. Ellen worked with E.W. from the start.
She wrote feature stories for the Detroit and Cleveland papers on
local people, places and events. The London-born Ellen was placid
but highly intelligent and maturely wise. She was one of the first

women college graduates in the United States, completing her work at Knox College in Illinois before the Civil War.

Ellen accepted the world as it was but E.W. steadfastly tried to shape and change it. Ellen—Miss Scripps, as she was known—was a private woman who loved books, solitude and reflection. She sought no publicity, wealth or other form of public attention, although they seemed to follow her. Ellen lived well, but she gave away virtually all of her wealth. She wrote her brother long, loving letters throughout both their lives, patiently counseling him as Scripps faced his most difficult problems. In turn, he poured out his soul to her.

Today, the name Scripps appears throughout the San Diego area—on medical and scientific institutions, schools, museums and parks. Ellen began most of this philanthropy: the Scripps Institution of Oceanography, Scripps Memorial Hospital, Scripps Clinic and Research Foundation, Scripps Metabolic Clinic, La Jolla Sanitarium, local libraries, nursing quarters, and other gifts. Ellen founded Scripps College for Women, which later became Claremont College. Her funds came from stock in the newspapers, investments and her inheritance from E.W.

Ed remembers his great-aunt as "very smart and very skinny." She was always dignified but hard of hearing. He recalls that, when Ellen broke her hip in a fall, E.W. immediately bought her a Rolls-Royce with a special lift for her wheelchair. She had a chauffeur. Ellen kept collections of fine books in her La Jolla basement. It was actually a fireproof vault because her earlier library had burned down. Some books from the first library were saved. Several were rare four-volume and larger sets. Ellen herself financed some of the rare books on birds. Ellen lived to be ninety-five and, before she died in 1932, made the cover of *Time* magazine in a story about her philanthropy.

E.W.'s sisters, Annie and Virginia, also were his confidantes. Annie supported her brother for years with loving letters but she was crippled with rheumatoid arthritis. She stayed in the background. Annie died in California at fifty-one in 1898.

"Miss Virginia," as she was called, was cut from a different cloth than Ellen or Annie. The redhead was known around the San Diego area as an eccentric. Virginia was a maiden lady with the mouth of a rough-cut rancher. She taught Sunday school at La Jolla's St. James-by-the-Sea Church. One Sunday, as the story goes, Virginia was holding class but couldn't hear her own voice because a construction crew was working on the church outside. Virginia marched out and asked the workmen to stop but they ignored her. Finally, she hollered: "God damn it! Stop that noise! I'm trying to teach the Lord's Prayer!"

During another class, a car continually backfired outside. Virginia stomped out and shouted at the driver: "What the hell do you think you're doing? Don't you know we're trying to pray inside?"

Ed recalls a story told to him by his mother. Virginia was riding with several ladies in a car. One of her guests was rather sassy and kept nudging Virginia with her elbow. In exasperation, Virginia removed her hat pin and stuck the lady in her air-blown bra. The startled lady was quickly deflated.

Virginia detested litterbugs. She often walked around La Jolla in the morning picking up papers and cussing men for spitting tobacco juice on the sidewalks. Friends said Virginia loved dominoes, singing, dancing and swearing—not necessarily in that order.

Privately, Virginia was a soft touch. She loaned money to almost anyone who asked. She sent food baskets to the poor and performed many other works of charity.

But, oh, how stubborn that woman was! Once a visiting friend was about to depart on a train home to Illinois. As the train prepared to pull out, the visitor remembered that she had forgotten one of her suitcases. Virginia took the other suitcase, marched out to the track, and sat herself on top of it in front of the locomotive. The engineer told her to get out of the way. Virginia wouldn't budge. Then he told her to get the hell out of the way. Virginia apparently replied in kind because the engineer was in a state of shock until his passenger returned and Virginia waved him onward. Some people said Virginia thought she had a divine right to swear.

Virginia took a nip of whiskey now and then. Some questioned how a churchgoing woman could do that. Virginia explained that she was of pure Scotch–Irish blood.

Virginia died in 1921 in London during a world tour. Friends said her last words were: Keep La Jolla clean!

If E.W. had few close friends, his disquisitions and other writings took the place of such companionship. They represent the soul of the man—as he saw it. The essays were not written for publication in the patriarch's lifetime. They were sent to friends and acquaintances since he clearly wished that others know about them. All the papers were ultimately bound into four sets of twelve volumes each to enlighten new generations of Scrippses and perhaps others. Ninety-two were published in the book, *I Protest*, edited by Oliver Knight (University of Wisconsin Press, 1966).

The Scripps Collection of E.W.'s disquisitions, correspondence and other personal papers—covering about 350,000 pages—was donated to Ohio University's Alden Library (Archives and Special Collections) by grandson Charles E. Scripps in 1988. Scripps is board chairman of the E.W. Scripps Company of Cincinnati as well as chairman of the Scripps Trust.

It is unclear why grandson Charles did not make the papers public for sixty years, since E.W. asked that they remain private only until 1951 or twenty-five years after his death. It is also uncertain whether any sensitive material has been retained by the Scripps Company or family officers, particularly papers which relate to E.W.'s split with his son Jim and the patriarch's trust. Such material, if it exists, would be important in better explaining the division of the business and family.

Ed has spent considerable time studying his grandfather's disquisitions and files. He explains that material which E.W. believed and did not believe are mixed together, making it virtually impossible to know what Scripps really thought on many subjects. The classic example is E.W.'s sympathy for socialism, which contradicts his entrepreneurial individualism and, indeed, his own autocracy. As a young man managing newspapers, the grandson gave up on this material as too unreliable. He instead went to the Cleveland public library and read the files of the Cleveland *Press* to better understand E.W. Ed says he found E.W., the editor and publisher, in the news columns of the *Press* itself—creative, condensed, human-interest reporting at its best. He recalled a letter which the old man had written to his father in the last stages of Jim's life. The letter told Jim to forget the disquisitions and files. E.W. said a newspaper owner's life boiled down to this: "Obey the Ten Commandments and make fifteen percent cash divisible net profit (on gross business) each year."

Those gold coins which E.W. carried in his pockets had more significance than anyone realized. They were to multiply into a multibillion-dollar empire. The sweeping expansion would come, however, at a price.

Ed carries a ten-dollar gold piece in his wallet as he walks the veranda of his Virginia home. He says it has nothing to do with his grandfather. But, of course, it does. It reminds him of the old man every day of his life.

CHAPTER

2

E.W.'S BIG BOOTS

Jim Scripps came of age at seventeen. In 1903 E.W. appointed his eldest son manager of his ranch and other properties at Miramar. Jim was also to account for his father's personal expenditures. It was no small job. E.W. employed scores of workers. New citrus trees were planted in groves. Eucalyptuses were set down as wind-breakers. Water pipelines and the car fleet needed repair. The horse stables had to be cleaned. Jim hired and fired, paid the workers and settled accounts. And the old man could spend a truckload of gold coins on his personal expenses over a single month.

If the job was big, so was Jim. He was already over six feet tall and weighed 185 pounds. The strapping young man dressed like a rancher—a wide-open shirt collar with khaki pants and work boots.

Jim was intelligent, decisive, all business.

E.W. had already designated Jim as his successor in personal letters and business memos. The old man planned that his son soon serve stints as an executive on several of his newspapers and then

31

James G. Scripps,
E.W.'s firstborn son, in
Cincinnati, where he
was directing the fam-
ily business circa 1912.

assume command of all his Western papers—from Denver to California and Washington.

In 1908 Jim married Josephine Stedem, a nurse he had met three
years earlier while recuperating from a difficult tonsil operation in
Cincinnati. Josephine, an attractive brunette of solid character and
poise, came from a large farm family near Champaign, Illinois. The
unannounced nuptials took place in a Cincinnati Presbyterian
church. The two had planned the wedding for several months, but
Jim was skittish about an announcement lest it cause any interference from E.W. He was particularly concerned since his bride was
about ten years older than himself.

As the day approached when Josephine was to meet the family,

Jim's anxiety grew. But as soon as E.W. and the family met her, they approved of Josephine. She shared their pride in family as well as E.W.'s long avowal of professional and personal responsibility.

E.W.'s second son, John Paul, was two years younger than Jim. He was a diligent young man and dutifully entered the newspaper business as a reporter. But he made a mistake in E.W.'s judgment. John, despite strong opposition from his father, married Edith McRae only a month after he became twenty-one. Everyone in the Scripps family knew what E.W. thought of the McRae sisters—not much. E.W. wouldn't attend the Detroit wedding.

About four years after his marriage, John became ill. Doctors were unsure what was wrong with him. The young husband returned to Miramar from his news duties in Cleveland for a rest. Doctors finally concluded that John had serious inflammation of his heart valves. The physicians were not optimistic. Some described the illness as terminal. E.W. was silent when the grim diagnosis was reached. John began slipping into a coma. E.W., in a last desperate hope to see some improvement in John's condition, went to see his son. It was to no avail. John died on April 22, 1914.

Robert was the youngest son, four years junior to Jim. He too defied his father over a McRae daughter, Helen. Bob had written the young woman a hot-blooded love poem and, when confronted about it by his father, confessed he had written the poem. Bob was not yet twenty-one and the old man was dead set against his marrying before that time. He told his son in no uncertain terms to back off. Furious at E.W., Bob left home and took a job in the oil fields near Bakersfield, California. He drifted from one roughneck outpost to another.

About a year later, Bob returned home under the watchful eye of E.W. He was still mooning for Helen. The young man spent most of his time loafing. He dabbled in poetry and played some tennis. To get Bob moving, E.W. sent him on a tour of the Far East—from Hawaii to Australia, Japan and other stops. Bob poured out more poetry but fortunately mailed it back only to his family. When he returned, Helen had married someone else. E.W. was delighted and Bob returned to his former lazy days and poetry.

In 1916, a tall brunette, Margaret "Peggy" Culbertson, began to visit Miramar as a guest. She was a pleasant young woman, the daughter of a Pasadena businessman. About six months later, in 1917, she and Bob were wed. Members of the Scripps family said it was an arranged marriage. If E.W. was relieved, he didn't show it. He wrote to Bob a month after the wedding: "I have told you several times that you need waking up. You haven't gone to sleep. You've never been awake . . .

"During this time, forget there is such a thing as poetry . . . Close the book of dreams for the time being; stop philosophizing."

The loss of his sons John Paul and Edward Wyllis McLean had wounded the old man deeply. He sought a successor with real strength. Of his surviving sons, Bob was the weaker. Jim was unquestionably the growing power in the family. That is why the old man sent him to Cincinnati in 1907 to run the central office. It was only a matter of time, E.W. told himself, before he could retire— that meant less work, not quitting—and devote more time to Miramar and the ocean voyages he loved. He announced his retirement only a year later.

Jim was twenty-one years old when E.W. installed him as the chief in Cincinnati. The young man had already helped launch Scripps's papers in Sacramento and Fresno. The Fresno *Tribune* was really Jim's baby, but E.W. replaced him when the financial outlook became shaky. Nevertheless, Jim had absorbed a lot of practical business sense and become a very knowledgeable, tough businessman— even shrewder and much more decisive than E.W.

The old man's decision to give Jim his power of attorney and send him to Cincinnati was well thought out. He wanted to see not only how his son worked with his top men but how he handled the power attached to the top job.

Jim did well. The older men noted that Jim had no desire to wield his authority indiscriminately nor did he ever demean anyone. He asked the right questions and deferred to wiser heads. The judgment on Jim was that he showed a good combination of directness, quickness and maturity.

Jim sold the St. Louis *Star-Chronicle* and closed the Kansas City

Cincinnati home of the James G. Scripps family during the years when James headed the family business.

World, two of the chain's longest and biggest moneylosers. He also folded or sold other bleeding sisters—the Nashville *Times*, Toledo *Times* and Columbus *Citizen*. E.W., who had vacillated about these weaklings for years, was delighted.

Jim detested the cold, mushy Cincinnati winters and let his father know about it. E.W. recalled his son to live and work at Miramar. Jim built a house there and by 1913 was earning $30,000 a year plus what E.W. referred to as an "increment"—a lump-sum monetary payment or stock bonus in the family newspapers. E.W. sometimes approved bonuses for his son of more than $200,000 in a single year. That was an extraordinary amount of money in those days. Jim was becoming a rich young man.

Meantime, Jim and Josephine had four children—Edward W., Jr., Josephine, James G., Jr., and Ellen. The parents were delighted with their brood. Ed, the eldest, remembers those days:

"My father always gave us time. He would get down on the floor with us and explain how trains and other toys worked. Even when he had to go on the road, he returned with presents for everyone. He also enjoyed taking us on car trips, to the beach at Del Mar, and he would often join when we played games. He was very much a family man. My father had only two interests—family and work. He fished

Ed Scripps, age 6, at the time
his father and family were
stationed in Cincinnati.

and hunted a little but had no interest in an outside social life. He
also liked motorcycles and that is how I got hooked on them.

"Dad would sometimes kid my mother, saying she was pigeon-
toed. I remember how both used to smile about it. Both considered
the words very endearing. It was a private thing between them.

"My mother and father ran a very open household. We talked
about everything. My parents were very loving people, especially to
each other. But the affection stopped when we misbehaved badly.
My father spanked me once for yelling in the house. He held me
over his knees and used a hair brush.

"We loved grandfather. I never heard my parents say a single word
against him. I can't remember one instance of unpleasantness
among my parents and grandfather. The only time they ever disagreed was when my mother wanted us to spend more time in school
while grandfather thought more energy should be put into outside
activities. I can't remember any harsh words about it. Nor can I recall

him using any argumentative words with me. He was solicitous about me, my brother and sisters. I developed a deep love for both my father and grandfather. I respect their memory to this day."

Meantime, the clouds of World War I broke over Europe in 1914. America questioned whether it should enter the war. E.W. believed he needed both his sons at home, not in military service, to run his business. As if the war were not enough to shake him up, daughter Nackey eloped with his male secretary, Tom Meanley. E.W. was livid. She was only eighteen.

E.W. attempted through his Washington contacts to get both sons exempted from the draft. Exemptions were given to men working in essential services, which included newspaper publishing. But Jim and Bob wanted to serve. The old man roared out of retirement and not only sought to keep his sons on the job but named himself the newspapers' policy czar. After a meeting with his top men in Washington, E.W. declared he wanted to alert the American people that the country was being led into the war and serious problems were involved. He ordered that certain stories, citing the dangers of such a conflict, be carried on the Scripps's front pages. Some editors and Jim were furious. E.W. was usurping their editorial privilege. Once America entered the war, however, the editorial conflict was resolved. E.W. had no more reservations.

E.W. met with Jim and Bob for about a week to straighten out their differences. All appeared appeased. The old man was already looking past the war. He virtually decided that all three would lead the company in the future as a triumvirate. Jim would run the business side and Bob would become editorial chief. Then suddenly Bob, in spite of his exemption, volunteered and was inducted into the Army as a private.

Tom Sidlo, an attorney for the Cleveland *Press*, then went to Secretary of War Newton Baker. Sidlo was a member of Baker's firm Baker and Sidlo, which represented the Scripps paper. Bob was subsequently discharged as an essential member of the civilian war effort. Government officials indicated that President Wilson himself made the decision. Wilson never denied it. Bob became the papers' editor-in-chief in Washington.

Jim's case was different than Bob's. He was virtually indispensable to the running of his father's company. Hearst's Los Angeles *Evening Record* supported a draft deferment for Jim and he eventually received one. Hearst and the Scripps' chain competed in many cities.

Then the two brothers really went to war—against each other. The fratricidal conflict was to last until Jim died. The battle was long, sickening and divided the family forever.

Jim and his family had returned to live in Cincinnati where he could be on top of everything at headquarters. He pulled Bob back from Washington, believing his brother was too inexperienced to be editor-in-chief.

Bob and Jim bickered incessantly. Finally, the brothers met their father in Miami to see what accommodation could be arranged. They chewed over their differences for four days. The result was a three-sided stone wall. Nothing was concluded.

Jim maintained that Bob did not have the intellectual maturity to direct the editorial side of the business. Bob constantly talked social revolution to solve labor problems. E.W. was concerned about Bob but he also asked himself why Jim so often forced a confrontation with his brother. Was Jim becoming too big for his britches?

Jim's objections to Bob's taking the top editorial slot were not unreasonable. He argued that Bob needed seasoning on several papers before assuming leadership of all of them. E.W. did not agree. He insisted that Bob should learn everything he needed from him. After all, E.W. maintained, he had already taught Jim everything he knew. Bob remained editor-in-chief although he had virtually no authority.

Nor could Jim easily forget what E.W. had written to Bob earlier: "I believe you have disqualified yourself for any but a menial position in my affairs."

The old man felt betrayed by his sons' infighting. He suffered a stroke in 1917 and was never the same man again. This proved significant in how the rest of the family viewed his professional and personal decisions. E.W.'s subsequent erratic behavior gave them reason to question his state of mind.

James G. and Josephine Stedem Scripps and their children, from left: Ed, Josephine L., Jim, Ellen Browning Scripps, at Miramar, circa 1916.

By 1916, after fewer than eight years as company chairman, Jim had increased revenues by nearly 100 percent, while the total circulation of the Scripps papers soared to over one million copies a day. Those figures demonstrated that Jim was abiding by the old man's dictum—make fifteen percent clear cash profit a year.

E.W. was moving behind the scenes. With the help of lawyers, the old man was secretly drafting a living trust to perpetuate the organization's "soul." By that, E.W. meant his lifelong commitment to the underdog, the poor, the common man—dedication to public service. Scripps was creating a holding company whereby the controlling stock, composed of his and Ellen's shares, would be bound together. His will was being redrafted, incorporating the holding company into a living trust which would be secure for one or two generations.

Jim effectively countermanded the old man's instructions that

Bob be given more power. He promoted Byron Canfield, chief of N.E.A., to become assistant chairman, effectively removing Bob as his Number Two man. The only way that E.W. could change Jim's decision was to remove Jim from the top job. He was not about to do that. But the old man did warn Jim that he was still the head man, meaning E.W. could withdraw his power of attorney and Jim would become only a straw man. This sword always hung over Jim's head but he counted on his exceptional job performance to sway his father's decision-making.

Jim had been protecting himself from whatever action E.W. might take. His incremental stock ownership, in lieu of company bonuses, in five West Coast newspapers grew to the point that he controlled the papers when his stock holdings were combined with those of executive friends.

E.W. then made his first big move against Jim. He slashed his son's power of attorney, limiting it to the business interests of the company's twenty-two newspapers, United Press and N.E.A. Then, in a truly stunning decision, E.W. granted Bob power of attorney over his personal matters—family trusts, estates, stocks and other affairs. Jim would no longer have a voice in his increments or stock bonuses. Bob would not only set those figures but act as his father's agent in company business affecting the old man's personal interests.

E.W. left no doubt in Jim's mind as to why he acted. The old man was saying that Bob had more concern for the "soul" of the organization—public service—than Jim did. Moreover, E.W. wrote to Jim that he wanted to teach his son a lesson: he was still the Great Teacher and supreme authority of the company.

The old man was acting in self-righteous fashion. He was accusing Jim of placing profit above soul and implicitly assailing him for instituting such a policy. E.W. really wanted it both ways—a specific large profit but putting public service first.

Jim was shocked but defiant. Bob was editor-in-chief but Jim believed that he was still the boss. He decided not to place his company stock in his father's living trust.

There has long been speculation within the Scripps family about E.W.'s strokes and their possible effects on later decisions, such as his trust. Josephine, Jim's wife, knew E.W. well. She maintained that E.W.'s three strokes between 1917 and his death in 1926 changed his behavior significantly. She said he became a Jekyll and Hyde. Contrary to his earlier forceful character, she said E.W. became very insecure. He was marked by insecurity for the rest of his life.

In the spring of 1920, Jim decided it was time to go his own way. He wrote his father that he and Bob were incapable of working as a team. He wanted to step down as chairman and go into some other business. E.W. suggested that Jim stay on another year and carefully think out his future.

E.W. retreated within himself, analyzing his sons' characters and abilities over and over again. Upset and suspicious of many people, the old man's moods swung from depression to despair. His physicians became concerned and warned that he could suffer another stroke.

Throughout these long soul-searching days, E.W. kept a somber diary. He reflected critically on both sons, accusing them of being drunkards. He also saw Jim as selfish and Bob as a fool.

Grandson Ed now reflects on those times and what he knew and learned about them. He says Bob was known as a heavy drinker. Ed recalls Bob getting drunk and smashing up his grandmother's car. But Ed denies that his father Jim was a drunkard. "We were a nondrinking family. Neither my mother nor sisters even drank. My brother and I also never took a drink until we began to do so socially much later in life.

"My mother was a very religious woman and never would have accepted my father drinking heavily or getting drunk. It was out of the question and, as a matter of fact, I never saw my father drinking around the house or drunk. To my knowledge, my father never went to bars.

"We all heard stories about company executives getting drunk when they were at various meetings. That was the macho way in those days. My father attended such meetings and I suppose there may have been times when he had several drinks. But it was completely out of character for him to get drunk. I don't believe it."

In April of 1920, Jim and E.W. held an emergency meeting.

A family gathering on the porch of the beach house at Del Mar. From the left: Ed, Lillian J. Baker, Elsie Scull, Josephine, Jim holding Ellen, Josephine L., young Jim, Mrs. Holtzsinger, Nackie Scripps.

Soaring newsprint prices and a paper shortage had sent some papers into a nose-dive, splashing them in red ink, and the old man blamed Jim. Jim responded that profits would fall even more because dual management with Bob was not working.

E.W. became concerned about the future of the organization. The big losses would never be halted as long as the brothers refused to communicate or work together. The old man decided that he would finally have to choose between them, and he chose Bob. Although Jim was a far superior businessman, he was difficult to control, while Bob was putty in the old man's hands.

E.W. summoned Bob and Roy Howard to Miramar on urgent business. When the two arrived, the old man told them that they would henceforth run the company. The three signed a contract.

Scripps delayed breaking with Jim. He wrote to his son saying he should continue as chairman at a salary of $36,000 a year, do chores of a "general" nature, and retain all his stock. None of that stock

could, however, be sold as long as E.W. lived. At the same time, E.W. offered to buy out Jim's stock for $1 million. His son declined. The old man, angry and fearful, was contradicting himself.

In June, about two months after making his decision to break with Jim, E.W. delivered to Bob a memo and a revised document giving Bob full power of attorney. He and Howard were replacing Jim. Howard was being transferred from the presidency of United Press to the chairmanship of the Scripps's board. Bob was editor-in-chief and of equal stature. The new firm was named Scripps-Howard. Dual management had prevailed.

Jim walked away with seven Western newspapers—the Los Angeles *Record*, Portland *News*, Sacramento *Star*, San Francisco *News*, Seattle *Star*, Spokane *Press* and Tacoma *Times*. He was accompanied by local executives whose stock support allowed Jim to take control of those papers. The Dallas *Dispatch* and Denver *Express* later joined Jim's fledgling chain.

Ed, who was ten years old at the time, recalls the split: "Although some people claim that my father and grandfather sometimes exchanged strong words, I don't think that's true. Not in this case or others. I can't recall a single instance when my father may have used a derogatory expression to or about my grandfather. He would have indicated that in our frank family discussions.

"My father and grandfather disagreed at times as longtime associates and even relatives do in any business. But that didn't make them unfriendly rivals. I think my father saw my grandfather as having one important flaw. Grandfather felt no one knew as much strategy as he did when facing newspaper problems. That caused most of the differences between father and son.

"My father ran the company for twelve years. When he took over in 1908, the concern was netting $300,000 a year. When he left in 1920, the company was making ten times that much, or about $3 million a year. My father had great foresight and helped the company make enormous progress."

Jim caught influenza which later developed into pneumonia. He became so weak that he couldn't get out of bed. His condition worsened and he lapsed in and out of a coma. Finally, in early January of 1921, just six months after the split with his father, Jim died. He was only thirty-four years old. His wife and children were grief-stricken. So were E.W. and Nackie, who blamed her husband for their son's death.

Shortly before Jim died, E.W. closeted himself in his study and wrote a disquisition about Jim. It appears to reflect better than any other source the old man's innermost personal appraisal of his son. It also foreshadowed the break between Jim's wife, Josephine, and E.W. The passages are as much a reflection of the old man as they are of Jim. E.W., in agonizing sorrow because he saw so much of himself in his son, tried to purge his soul in these words: ". . . Jim was a fighter. He was one of that kind of men to whom life would probably be dull even to the point of being unendurable were it not for antagonism. My son was a man whom William James would have called 'tough-minded.' He was not a sentimentalist. He dearly loved to view prizefights. His play was rough play. He enjoyed business because he enjoyed life and struggle.

"His disposition was not avaricious or miserly. Often in his talks with me, he has protested that he did not value money for the sake of money, and that all he found interesting in business was 'playing the game.'

"... He married young, and had four children. He was a good husband and a devoted father. He loved to play with his children . . . and their toys.

"From the time even before he got into his teens, his was a remarkable personality. At times, child as he was, he had all the gravity and maturity of a middle-aged man . . .

"He was never happy when away from his home and children; and whenever he was away from his family, he received daily telegraphic messages concerning his children. His anxiety on their account was continuous . . .

"Jim was a man of two distinct personalities. My older brother James, if he had few friends, had no enemies. He hated no one. It was impossible for him to harbor any enmities or resentments. The other brother never forgot or forgave an injury. Jim was a good enough hater—too good a hater, I thought.

"Jim was a born financier. He was always careful of his money, even as a child. He liked to 'trade'—that is to say, he liked to measure his wits with other boys and men. He gloried in getting the best of the bargain.

"... I felt pretty sure that as he grew older and developed mentally, he would take pleasure in the business of moneymaking. By the time he had thrown aside his books, I had become convinced of the uselessness of my attempting to teach him or train him to do anything or be anything but that which was in accordance with his natural bent.

"He was only fifteen years of age when I gave him his liberty—that is to say, I discharged him from his obligations to me as a minor. At the same time I turned over to him the management and control of my household and personal affairs and expenditures. He was fully competent to take over this work and he enjoyed it . . . I was as willing to trust him with any minor business affairs as I would have been to trust a man ten years older.

"When he was only a few weeks past twenty-one years of age, I put him in charge of my central business office, and only a few months later, I gave him my full power of attorney; and for a number of years, for reasons of my own, I permitted him to exercise absolute control over all of my financial transactions, though I would never permit him to exercise control—full control or even partial control—over the editorial department of my newspaper properties . . . Occasionally there would be some matter in which we strongly differed, but always on such occasions Jim submitted to my absolute control.

"Beginning in his early life, I began transferring property to Jim . . . I made considerable additions to Jim's fortune . . . I treated him as a partner . . . He told me that he had obtained a fortune by that time (in his mid-twenties) . . . larger than he would ever have occasion to need.

"Beginning even in his years of childhood, I had endeavored to impress upon Jim that, as he was the eldest of my children, he was eventually to be the head of the family and the head of the business, and that he must consider himself responsible for the affairs of his mother and his brothers and sisters. Frankly and frequently, Jim told me that he did not desire this position—that he wanted to have only the responsibility for his own affairs and to have no other responsibilities than those pertaining to his own immediate family.

"Jim was always frank and outspoken. To the best of my recollection, Jim never told me a lie or acted a lie. He gave me just as thoroughly to understand that he did not propose to be the keeper of his brothers and sisters as I gave him to understand that he must do so in duty to me.

"Jim was truthful, brutally truthful. Came the time when I and my son found ourselves openly and frankly in opposition and antagonistic. Jim gave me no excuse for thinking or hoping that he would (any) longer be submissive to me.

"Jim had become wealthy. He was a millionaire in his own right.

Still, his wealth was perhaps not one-fifth as large as would eventually at my death be his share of the estate. He recognized this, as I did, and we talked together plainly on this subject. The time had come when it was no longer endurable for Jim to submit to the commands of any other man, even his own father.

"There was a contest lasting for several years—lasting in its acute form for nearly a year. During all this time, I had a divided mind with regard to what I wanted my son to do. While the idea of an open rupture between us two was extremely repugnant to me, I felt that I would suffer even more keenly if my son should be utterly subservient to anyone else, even to his father. I felt that I would prefer to be defied by my son, and even antagonized and injured by my son, than that a son of mine should be soft and weak.

"I am sure that he enjoyed this strife.

". . . I was a strong man and an able man, and Jim knew it. There was no occasion for his having pity, then, or sympathy for me.

"Jim had a different code of ethics from my own. There were things that he would do and think right that I would not do because I thought they were wrong; and doubtless there were many things

A buggy ride for the family picnic at Miramar, 1920, the summer before the death of Jim Scripps.

that I would do and think right that Jim would not do because he would not think them right . . . I do not think that he would have done at any time different from what he did do had he felt sure that death was just before him.

". . . He has left behind a family of children that any man might be proud of. He has enjoyed a successful career, and he died almost suddenly . . .

"If this disagreement—call it quarrel, if one will—between father and son must result in any sort of unhappiness, it is going to be the father who will suffer and not the son. So why should my affection for my son cause me to grieve at his death?

"I believe that if I had died and Jim lived, Jim would have suffered no remorse; nor would there have been any occasion for him to have suffered any remorse. Jim obeyed his nature, and I am not sorry today because Jim's nature was such as it was.

"Perhaps I am as 'tough-minded' as my son was 'tough-minded.'

"A fighting man is fortunate if he can die fighting in the heat of battle . . ."

Editor & Publisher, the bible of the newspaper industry, carried an obituary about Jim on January 15, 1921. It said in part:

> "The death of James G. Scripps . . . ended one of the most remarkable careers in the history of American newspaper work. He was the responsible head of the great Scripps newspaper organization for twelve years, conducting its affairs with conspicuous success yet was only thirty-four years of age when he died."

The obit quoted associates praising Jim's work but he probably would have appreciated these two lines more than the eulogies: "Personally, he was of the simplest possible tastes . . . He held an amused contempt for what is commonly called 'society' and refused to have anything to do with it." The article referred to Jim's plain rancher's clothes and his love for hunting and fishing.

Jim's funeral service was held in his home. Josephine and her four children sat near the casket. Ed, then eleven years old, recalls that mourners overflowed the large room and chairs had to be set up in the corridor outside. The Episcopalian minister summed up Jim as an exemplary family man with one of the country's most creative business minds.

Jim was buried in the family plot at Greenwood cemetery south of San Diego near Chula Vista. Ed remembers that his mother and his brother and sisters struggled to mask their emotions as eight business colleagues carried the casket up a cemetery hill. E.W. sat home and brooded.

Nackie and E.W. clashed more often after Jim's passing. Nackie continued to insist that E.W.'s fights with Jim contributed to her son's early death. E.W., more grief-stricken than Nackie realized, was angered by her harping. For the next five years, until his death, E.W. and Nackie had an off-again, on-again relationship. They exchanged caring letters one month and bitter recriminations the next.

For a single day, on September 16, 1922, E.W. became a boy again. He arrived at Newport News, Virginia, to see the launching of his new yacht, the *Ohio*. He was dumping his much smaller twelve-year-old vessel, the *Kemah* (an Indian word for "rain on the face") for a sleek new 172-foot ship with every modern convenience, including a bathtub built to E.W.'s large specifications. The yacht, with a twenty-six-foot beam, drafting eleven feet, cost $350,000, ten times more than the *Kemah*, and had a range of more than 10,000 miles with 700 horsepower, capable of eleven knots. It had two large staterooms as well as six smaller guest rooms, a big dining room and library. There were quarters for up to thirty crew members.

As the *Ohio* slid into the water amid cheers from bystanders, E.W. was already planning a world cruise. He would visit the Orient and might even try to write a second novel. The first was a bust. Nackie rejected his invitation to join him, and derided his idea of bringing any grandchildren along.

Meanwhile, all was not well between Bob Scripps and Roy Howard. Howard simply didn't believe that twenty-seven-year-old Bob, with little on-the-line experience to back him up, could cut it as a news executive. The old man told Howard that he, E.W., was still the boss and to shut up. Howard did and E.W., with a yacht full of guests, set out on the *Ohio* for Hawaii, then plowed across the Pacific to Japan and, later, China. At Shanghai, Katherine Steelman, Dolla's former nurse, came aboard to say hello to her onetime employer. She was performing private duty in Shanghai. E.W., who had been suffering from colds and other illnesses on the voyage, immediately offered Steelman a free ride back home in return for becoming his private nurse and reader. She quickly accepted.

Steelman was a homely old maid and Nackie had nothing to fear in her. But when she heard about the nurse, she hit the roof with moans and groans that could be heard throughout Miramar. Nackie threatened to hang out all the family laundry in a divorce proceeding. The old man stubbornly refused to give up his nurse.

E.W. didn't return to the wails at Miramar. He holed up on Santa Catalina Island while the *Ohio* was overhauled. He planned another international excursion to escape Nackie's wrath. Before embarking, the old man arranged a complicated strategy to outwit his wife and family. Using a series of secret codes, he would send and receive messages from the home office in Cincinnati. Only a few executives at headquarters—and his sister Ellen—were to know where he was.

He sailed to the Caribbean and back to San Diego in March of 1924. Nackie agreed to come abroad although Miss Steelman was still on staff. The *Ohio* was to cruise the Atlantic coast to Baltimore. On the trip Nackie made peace and agreed to go on a Mediterranean cruise with her husband, but by the time they reached Baltimore, the two were fighting again.

The yacht needed more than a month's overhaul. Nackie decided to visit relatives in the Midwest and thus the confrontation ended. Nurse Steelman ministered to Scripps's aches at a hotel. The old man's doctors learned that, with Nackie aboard, E.W. was back to a quart of booze a day. They told him he was killing himself and ordered an indefinite separation from Nackie, who returned to Miramar.

In the summer of 1924, Scripps sailed for the Mediterranean, where he stopped at Gibraltar, Algeria and Tunisia. The yacht was overhauled again in Naples and E.W. revisited Rome during the stopover. However, the thrill of the first visit was gone. Via Egypt and the Suez Canal, the *Ohio* ultimately landed in Australia. The ship didn't return to San Diego until the spring of 1925. E.W. had not seen, written or heard from Nackie for more than nine months.

The *Ohio* embarked from San Diego after only a few days in port. E.W. had met with Bob to discuss business. His son's report was excellent: E.W. had a personal income of nearly $2 million a year, while the company was worth about $80 million. Scripps felt that, with such all-around good news, he should write Nackie. It had been nearly a year since the two communicated. His letter was warm. She returned the cordiality.

Scripps began to have serious breathing problems but he ordered the crew to head for the Canary Islands. While underway, he began writing disquisitions on death and forgiveness. After a stop in Spain, the *Ohio* headed for South Africa. E.W. and his Cincinnati staff were still playing their cat-and-mouse game with Nackie, Bob and everyone else. No one knew precisely where the old man and the *Ohio* were.

In Cape Town, Scripps was hot copy. His long, lonely voyages caused reporters to describe him as a "hermit" of the seas. E.W. had become a rich, international enigma. The yacht embarked for Liberia and arrived at Monrovia in March of 1926. Scripps took a sightseeing tour of the capital.

On the evening of March 12, 1926, E.W. had guests aboard the *Ohio* for dinner. During after-dinner drinks and conversation in the ship's library, he became ill. As the guests departed and Miss Steelman struggled to save his life, Scripps gagged, dry vomited, and fought for breath. He turned blue and made no response to the nurse's questions and requests. He slipped into unconsciousness. Resuscitation efforts failed. The giant of newspaperdom and indeed one of the most colorful Americans of the century was dead. He was seventy-one years old. Physicians from Liberia came aboard and confirmed that his death had been caused by apoplexy.

Scripps left a sealed envelope in the ship's safe. The letter inside, written in September of 1923, said that, if he became seriously ill, no member of his family or business associate should be notified until after his death. He requested to be buried at sea.

A family picnic at Miramar, 1920.

The Cincinnati office was informed by cable that Scripps had passed away and had left written instructions to be buried at sea. The headquarters replied that burial should be delayed until son Bob and others were notified. The *Ohio* waited but no word came for a full day. It was then decided to bury the old man as he had wished.

The yacht lifted anchor in Monrovia Bay and moved out to sea. The simple coffin was pried open and Scripps's body placed in canvas. The shroud was sewn and bound by rope. An American flag was attached to the canvas.

Jimmy Young, a young man hired by Scripps as a ship's clerk, wrote a brief, informal prayer. He recited it before the crew about 6:00 P.M. as the sun was falling over the African coast. The invocation closed with these words:

"God gave you. God takes you away. I cast you into the deep."

The ship's cannon fired a first salute. On the second pull of the cannon's lanyard, Scripps's body slid down into the waters and sank. Flowers were dropped on the waves as the cannon fired a third and final farewell.

Scripps died and was buried alone—without family or friend. Those in attendance were hired staff. A pile of gold coins, sequestered in his safe, now had no value for him. He died without a word from his son Bob or his associates in Cincinnati. It was an empty, perhaps even bitter ending.

The Scripps trustees sold the 1,200 acres of E.W.'s beloved Miramar to a developer in 1968 for $4.2 million. They balked at continued payment of the high taxes on the place.

The Maaco Corporation, a wholly owned subsidiary of Penn Central Company, has since paved over the land and constructed mass residential housing and an industrial complex. Shopping malls, supermarkets and giant parking lots span the once open landscape.

The new owners planned to preserve Scripps's forty-seven-room ranch house and make it into a museum like the Hearst estate at San Simeon. In 1972, however, the house was vandalized and looted of all its antiques. The structure was then razed.

Josephine, a daughter of E.W.'s son Jim, eventually owned Fanita Ranch. Miss Scripps stayed out of the news business and instead started a dairy and ran cattle at Fanita. When World War II erupted, she sold half the remaining 7,000 acres to the U.S. government for the army's Camp Elliott, now Tierrasanta. Josephine sold the remainder of Fanita in 1967. She then bought Hi-Hope Ranch, some twenty miles north near Oceanside. Josephine, who was an excellent mineralogist, died in 1992 at the age of eighty-one.

The *Ohio* was sold by the Scripps family in 1926 and had four private owners before the U.S. Navy bought the vessel in 1940. The navy renamed the ship *Turquoise* (PY–18), and used it as an antisubmarine patrol craft during most of World War II. The ship was subsequently sold by the United States to the Ecuadorian navy. The Ecuadorians ran the vessel aground and wrecked it in 1953 off the coast of Guayaquil.

No tombstone or monument records the old man's life. Perhaps there was one, the Cleveland *Press*, which held so much of E.W.'s blood, sweat and soul within its walls, but the *Press* was run into the ground and eventually sold to a Cleveland industrialist at a bargain-basement price. It collapsed and finally died. It was a tragic ending for what was once one of the country's leading dailies.

Eternity held no rest or peace for E.W. His mind, will, and corpse were to be resurrected from the sea in a public family fight.

3

SCRIPPS v. *SCRIPPS*

E.W. had set the mood for the battle. He met with Josephine on August 14, 1921. Twelve-year-old Ed Scripps heard loud voices coming from his grandfather's study. He was very surprised. Not only was it a drowsy Sunday morning but his mother was facing the old man.

The voices rose and fell as the hot noonday sun baked his grandfather's courtyard. The youngster strained to hear but he couldn't understand the words. He was certain, however, of one thing. That was his mother's voice and she had never sounded so upset.

Josephine had been with E.W. for two hours. Ed waited. He was concerned. Why hadn't his mother taken him with her? She had done so in other meetings with his grandfather. He was the man of the family now. His mother had told him that. She explained that he must grow up in a hurry to take his father's place.

Finally, the study was silent. Sooner or later, Ed reflected, the August heat made everything still. His mother walked toward him.

Josephine Stedem Scripps with her son, Ed. The death of her husband when Ed was 11 would mark the beginning of a legal battle with the Scripps estate that would last until Ed was 19.

Her brown eyes looked squarely at her eldest son. She put her arm on his shoulder and they walked home to Fanita Ranch in silence.

Mother and son together sat in their living room. Josephine spoke softly but the words were like thunder. She and her sons were about to go it alone in the news business—not join grandfather and Scripps-Howard. They were forming their own company with her late husband's seven newspapers—the Los Angeles *Record*, San Francisco *News*, Sacramento *Star*, Seattle *Star*, Spokane *Press*, Tacoma *Times*, and Portland *News*. (Jim had obtained control of the Dallas *Dispatch* and Denver *Express*, but they were not part of this.)

Jim had not owned these newspapers outright but controlled them through his personal stock holdings as well as agreements with Scripps executives who also owned stock in the papers. E.W. had reminded Josephine that Jim was to resell any stock holdings to him. She replied that, since the stock was left totally in her name in Jim's will, it was now hers. She added that there was no written agreement that Jim or she must resell the stock to E.W. Josephine reminded the patriarch that, under the decade of her husband's

Ed vacationing at Mir-
amar on his favorite
motorcycle, circa
1928.

guidance, the value of the Scripps papers increased from $3 million
to about $20 million. Simultaneously, profit rose from about
$300,000 a year to $3 million. She then pointed out that E.W. had
not fulfilled a written agreement with his son which stipulated that
Jim would receive half of the papers' profit growth in addition to
their annual financial gains. Josephine was polite, but she made it
plain that E.W. had reneged on a contract.

The old man insisted that Josephine return the "outlaw" papers
to his fold. He offered to pay her $1 million for her husband's stock
in the five papers. He also reminded her that she would receive Jim's
inheritance—almost five percent of the entire organization. Jim
owned part of each paper through an "increment agreement" with
his father, whereby E.W. paid his son stock bonuses for good work.
In talking with Josephine, E.W. also promised to leave his two young
grandsons, Ed and Jim, $1 million each in his will if the "outlaw"
papers came back to Scripps-Howard.

E.W. then berated the widow, particularly her business ability: "Josephine, you belong in the lowest class of kindergarten, while I am a postgraduate of the (business) university . . ."

The patriarch appeared to refer to a meeting which he had with Josephine seven months earlier, six weeks after Jim died. The widow had told E.W. that she wanted to try running the papers herself for a year. Josephine felt that her husband would have wanted it that way. There was another reason, perhaps her strongest motive. She opposed E.W.'s wish that her two sons remain at Miramar and be trained by him. He had written Jim before he died: ". . . My affection for your children is great and I know they have greatly enjoyed their free association with me. I believe that they will gain greatly by, as I will enjoy greatly, their frequent visits to me . . . It will be a sad thing, Jim, for these your children to grow up and be estranged from me during the last years of my life.

"On the other hand, my affection for them being so great, it would be impossible for their intimate association with me not to result in their gaining much from my teaching and example."

Josephine abhorred E.W.'s "teaching and example" and, shortly after her husband's death, left Miramar with her family for a town house adjacent to San Diego's Balboa Park. She did not want to be dominated by E.W. and lived there for a year before returning to reside with daughter Josephine at Fanita Ranch. E.W. rarely visited the ranch. The widow questioned E.W.'s morality and ethics. She detested his heavy drinking and liberal outlook on sex. Above any and all considerations—including all the money and power that E.W. could offer them—she wanted her sons and daughters to live by strong Christian values and high moral standards. In polite language, as a mother, she told him precisely that in their meeting.

E.W. became angry. He retorted that Jim's defection with the "outlaw" papers had cost the company "several million dollars." He claimed the move had depreciated his stock by at least $1 million and other stockholders' shares by another million. Apparently close to nervous collapse, Scripps screamed that the defection had cost Josephine's own family $100,000 in depreciated stock value.

Then, in unmistakable language, Scripps threatened the widow:

"Now who ought to lose that money? Considering your children as my heirs, is it right that after the loss caused by their parents they should have equal standing with the others of my heirs?"

Josephine did not respond. She stared unbelievingly at the old man and the cruelty that spit from his mouth. The widow would not dignify his crude and ruthless bullying with a response. E.W. was learning that she was a strong-willed individual. She was not, as he was often given to say, another "foolish woman."

There were other reasons for Josephine's rejection of Scripps's offer.

First, John H. Perry, a longtime lawyer and associate of E.W., had jumped ship and joined Josephine. He was a large stockholder in her new firm. In July of 1921, about six months after Jim's passing, Perry told Josephine that E.W. had cooked up a deal whereby he would sell N.E.A., the Scripps feature-illustrations-comics syndicate, to himself for some $200,000, although it was worth at least $1 million. Perry described E.W.'s plan as a "robbery" of other stockholders.

Josephine was concerned because selling N.E.A. for a bargain-basement price would severely diminish her inheritance share. She saw the deal as an incestuous conspiracy. Josephine and her children were living on the dividends from their stock in the breakaway papers. She threatened to pull her papers out of N.E.A., leaving the service in financial difficulty, if E.W. did not halt the plan. She also warned that she might cut all her connections with the Scripps organization.

The scheme was not E.W.'s. It was the dubious brainchild of his son Bob and Roy Howard. The syndicate would actually be peddled to one of their associates, Earle Martin, for $150,000. Martin would become N.E.A.'s new president and would sell the service to all newspapers. The Scripps-Howard papers would receive a separate service. Bob and Howard predicted big profits. Despite Josephine's opposition, the Scripps trustees approved the N.E.A. deal.

Second, one of E.W.'s private memos was accidentally delivered to Josephine. It spoke of "iron-clad" provisions that required sons Jim and John Paul to return their increment stock to him. Josephine interpreted the memo to mean that E.W. felt his sons had betrayed their word and perhaps acted illegally in retaining the stock. The widow was very upset because E.W. appeared to be challenging her right to the stock and, therefore, her integrity.

A week later, after another meeting with E.W., Josephine formally broke with Scripps-Howard. She would pull out her seven papers, as well as Dallas and Denver, on January 1, 1922. Josephine was upset not only at the N.E.A. deal but the conviction that neither E.W. nor Bob was helping her. Josephine sincerely hoped that she was wrong about Bob.

She met with Bob about a month later on February 17, 1921. Josephine asked him to recommend three executors for her will. Bob suggested himself and two other men. Josephine then discussed personnel changes in her Denver and Dallas papers and was inclined to accept Bob's advice. Finally, she asked for input on who should be her company's chairman of the board. Bob, impressed by Josephine's desire to work hard for the papers, suggested that she herself become chairman. Bob also defended his plan to reorganize N.E.A. He did not discuss its bargain sale price. The conversation closed with Bob discussing Josephine's sons as his possible successors. This pleased the widow. Bob had handled Josephine gently to avoid her pulling her papers out of Scripps-Howard permanently.

Josephine left the meeting convinced that Bob was an ally. In her bereavement, she believed his friendship was one of the anchors of her life, a misapprehension that was to haunt her for the rest of her life. Bob would eventually treat Josephine more harshly than any individual that she had ever met.

On June 7, 1922, aboard his yacht *Kemah*, Scripps created a living trust in which he placed his entire estate (E.W. would gain all the income and control it as long as he lived). The document put all of the patriarch's business and other interests under Bob's sole direction. The Edward W. Scripps Trust was the most far-reaching legal instrument that E.W. had ever signed. By a few strokes of the pen, estranged from his wife and most of his family, the old recluse had cut off all but one of his children from most of his vast legacy. The estate was estimated at the time to be worth about $40 million. The trust was to terminate only after two successive generations—Bob's and his children's. The trust will probably end sometime around 2005, when twenty-eight grandchildren will inherit an estimated $1.5 billion.

Apart from the irreconcilable differences between Jim and Bob, E.W. concluded that his action would guarantee that public service would always be placed above profit in the future operation of his empire. Putting it in his grandiloquent language, to preserve the organization's "soul."

On June 26, 1922, less than three weeks after E.W. placed unprecedented power in Bob's hands, the old man wrote of deep reservations about his son in his diary:

> "I have never been certain as to Bob's motives during the past two or three years, or whether he had any motives.
>
> "Sometimes I have wondered whether or not he was shrewd enough minded to have recognized that the dispute developing between Jim and myself was likely to inure greatly to his (Bob's) advantage.
>
> "I really wanted to feel that in this respect he was something of a fool.
>
> "I would certainly be more unhappy than I am now if I should feel that all along Bob had been playing a very shrewd part in allowing developments to take their course without his being implicated."

E.W.'s erratic appraisal of Bob had already been demonstrated two years earlier in his diary entry of June 23, 1920. He wrote:

> ". . . In my recent talks with Bob (that is up to a week ago) I have told Bob that it was my intention that Jim should have the lion's share of my estate providing I could do this and at the same time secure to (sic) him (Bob) the permanent control of the newspapers."

In summing up his feelings about Bob and Jim in 1920, E.W. wrote:

"I really consider it probable that there will be litigation, perhaps between myself and my son Jim, during my lifetime, and certainly between my two sons after me."

In addition to Bob and his descendents, the trust bequeathed E.W.'s widow Nackie $60,000 a year and lifetime residence at Miramar. Daughter Nackey Meanley was left a $200,000 trust and a $30,000 annuity. Her survivors were to receive $1 million on termination of his living trust. Bob was crowned the family prince—sole trustee of the living trust and executor of E.W.'s estate.

E.W. not only contradicted himself in his treatment of Josephine and her family but was notably spiteful. In a somber meeting with the widow on January 12, 1921, less than a week after Jim died, E.W. promised Josephine that he would leave her in his will all the stock which he owned in her husband's papers. The old man wrote the promise in his diary.

Despite the solemnness of that moment, E.W. reneged on his pledge. Eight months after signing the living trust, the patriarch wrote an extraordinary letter to Josephine on March 4, 1923. In it, E.W. revealed that he had created the trust, naming Bob as trustee, and then unleashed one of the pettiest broadsides of his life:

"I have made proper provision in my trust for the immediate members of my family, exclusive of Dolla who is already provided for, but I have not made any provision for the children of either of my deceased sons. This (is) for various reasons, some of which will probably occur to you." (He was undoubtedly referring to the "outlaw" papers and Josephine's decision to remove her children from his influence.)

E.W. then tried to tempt Josephine: "Perhaps conditions will change. I do not know."

He couldn't resist a parting shot at her: "I do not now think so."

Josephine was shocked for two reasons. She understood that E.W. had had an unbreakable increment agreement with her husband that said Jim would be compensated for the growth of the company during his tenure as its chairman. The stock that he had received thus far did not come close to what her late husband and Josephine believed was due him. Second, E.W. had repeatedly promised in family meetings, letters and memos—and to her personally—that Jim's children would receive an inheritance from him.

Despite E.W.'s statement to Josephine that she would receive Jim's inheritance, almost five percent of the company's stock, the widow was not left a ten-dollar gold piece. Her four children, for whom E.W. so often professed "great affection," received not even a penny from the old Penny Papers. This was despite the fact that E.W. wished to be their teacher and his many promises to Jim, in conversation as well as written memoranda, about his eventual legacy. Josephine and the children now paid for Jim's unwillingness to bow before the throne. E.W.'s trust was a merciless act of uncommon vindictiveness.

When the old man died in 1926 without honoring the increment accord or leaving his grandchildren anything, Josephine hired lawyers to challenge the trust.

This was not the first time that the family had engaged in such a battle. James E. Scripps, E.W.'s brother, contested the will of brother George H. Scripps in 1900. George had left his newspaper stock to E.W. That fight was finally settled out of court in 1903 when E.W. exchanged George's one-third interest in the Detroit *News* for James E.'s stock in other newspapers.

Neither Josephine nor her son Ed was shocked. Jim had already warned them that he believed the old man to be mentally incompetent as a result of his strokes. No one in the family tried to prove this, although E.W. had virtually abandoned his wife and fled from the rest of the family. The old man's physicians also had told the family that he was ill and weak. Too much excitement could send the old man into a mental tailspin and kill him. The airing of the incompetency charges would have been a public embarrassment to the old man and the family. Josephine and young Ed were too loyal for that. The patriarch and the family came first.

Josephine carried another private heartache. Some seven months before Jim died, E.W. told him privately that one of the reasons that he had named Bob his editor-in-chief during World War I was

B.H. Canfield, center between Ed and his brother Jim. Canfield was a two-fisted crusader who joined Josephine Scripps in her newspaper venture.

because Jim's wife was "a German." He added that some Americans had raised the question of German-American loyalty to the United States. By naming Bob as editor-in-chief, E.W. said he barred the suspicion that the Scripps papers' early criticism of the war might be influenced by "a German woman." Josephine was not a German; she was a German-American who was born and raised in Illinois. Josephine was stunned by the tenor of the conversation when Jim related it to her, but never mentioned it again.

Josephine reflected on another sad aspect of her life. Over the previous five years, Nackie had often sided with Jim and Josephine in their disputes with her husband. When Jim died, Nackie was so distressed that she accused E.W. of being partly responsible for the deaths of their sons Jim and John Paul. However, despite claims to the contrary, Nackie changed after Jim's passing and the finalization of E.W.'s living trust. She sided with Bob and E.W. in virtually every decision. Nackie privately explained to Josephine that she had no choice. Bob was her only surviving son and E.W. had become her only link to family and friends because of his power.

In her will, Nackie wrote that she was not leaving any money to Josephine and her children because they had already been taken care of. Nackie saw Jim's papers as an inheritance rather than the result of his work. She left most of her legacy, perhaps as much as $3 million, to her daughters—Dolla, who was mentally retarded, and Nackey, who had remained close to her mother. She bequeathed the large family home in West Chester, Ohio, to Bob, who had been named as the executor of her will. In a very significant footnote, Nackie said that, if her daughter Nackey were dead at the time of her will's probate, Nackey's share should go to the daughter's children.

One reason for Josephine's decision to break with E.W. was apparent to few. Some of the Scripps executives loyal to Jim came to Josephine and said that, as Masons, they had taken an oath to help widows in need. They would join forces with her by committing their stock in the breakaway papers to her control. Thus, E.W. could no longer threaten her hold on the breakaway papers.

Josephine, because she held most of the stock and had long training by Jim, became chairwoman of the board of the new company—the Scripps-Canfield newspapers. Byron Canfield, who had been the West Coast editor of the Scripps papers, joined her and became the second largest stockholder in the new company. Canfield was a two-fisted fighter and crusader. Their first business headquarters was in Oakland. Attorney Jay Curts, a stockholder who made the choice, lived in nearby Piedmont. Later, the headquarters was transferred to Seattle, where Josephine moved with her children.

During this time, there were rumors that E.W. sent some of his executives to the West Coast asking Canfield and LeRoy Sanders, a veteran Scripps executive and stockholder in the breakaway papers, to sell him enough of their stock so that E.W. would control the papers and return them to his fold. Josephine was furious, although no one was ever able to prove the rumor. The episode reflected increasingly poor relations between E.W. and the widow. The old man was still outraged at the breakaway papers. E.W., who had owned some stock in all the breakaways, eventually exchanged his holdings for stock which Jim held in some of his papers.

Raising her children and running the company at the same time became too heavy a burden for Josephine. The widow devoted much time and training to son Ed, whom she expected would eventually take her place. However, Ed was not yet twenty-one and some of her partners were fighting. Ed recalls that Canfield developed a drinking problem. Josephine bought out both Canfield and Perry, who wanted money for other business ventures. The widow hired Milton McRae, longtime aide of E.W., as chairman. Nevertheless, various partners continued feuding. Josephine dismissed McRae and attempted to replace him with lawyer Curts. Sanders strongly objected. The widow bought Sanders's stock but not before he threatened not only the organization but the widow's entire estate.

Josephine's agreement with Sanders had a "deficiency clause." If her annual payments of $90,000 for his $900,000 worth of stock were not made on time, Sanders could foreclose on Josephine's entire estate. The widow claimed the clause was hidden in the agreement's fine print but she should have noted it. Sanders threatened to foreclose during the Depression but Josephine managed to come up with her annual payment.

Meanwhile, publisher Eugene MacLean of the San Francisco *News* resigned. Unless the company retained his twenty percent stock interest, Josephine and her other partners would lose control of the *News* and its sister paper, the Sacramento *Star*. MacLean sold his stock for $300,000 to Scripps-Howard and the breakaway papers were cut to five—in Los Angeles, Seattle, Spokane, Tacoma, and Portland. Earlier, Josephine had returned the Dallas *Dispatch* and Denver *Express* to E.W. She decided there were simply too many problems at both papers.

During these crises, Josephine turned to E.W. for stock proxy and other help. He sent back word through Bob: No!

Meantime, Josephine visited Scripps headquarters in Cincinnati to learn more about what was going on in the business and family.

She was surprised to discover that the partners still owed E.W. about
$200,000 for the stock that they held in the breakaway papers. The
widow was dismayed to hear rumors that Bob was drinking heavily
and chasing fast women with Roy Howard.

In 1928, two years after E.W.'s death, Josephine moved from
Fanita Ranch to the new company headquarters at Seattle to be near
her son Ed, who was working on the Seattle *Star*. She was about to
make a very dramatic move and wanted her eldest son at her side.
Ed had been a reporter on the *Star* and later worked in the paper's
circulation and advertising departments. The young man was
viewed by the editors and other executives as bright and hard
working. He had earlier held similar posts on the Spokane *Press*.

After forming her own company, Scripps-Canfield Newspapers, Josephine
moved her headquarters to Seattle, where Ed was already working on the
Star.

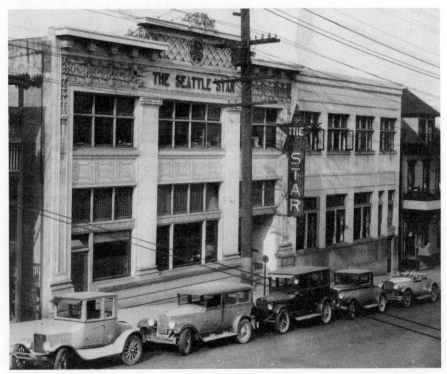

In the midst of her relocation to Seattle, Josephine made her move. She sued Bob as trustee and executor of E.W.'s trust. The widow sought to receive $6 million, which represented the increment (bonus for work) and profits agreement which E.W. had made with her husband for managing the company over a decade.

Judge Smith Hickenlooper, of the U.S. District Court for the Western Division of the Southern District of Ohio, ruled in July of 1928 that Josephine did not establish a binding or legal obligation between E.W. and Jim. Bob won the first battle, but the war had just begun.

Ed and brother Jim were still settling into their new headquarters, but Josephine was already moving to appeal the verdict. She had assembled a legal powerhouse led by Charles Evans Hughes, former U.S. Secretary of State and future Chief Justice of the Supreme Court, to challenge E.W.'s trust before the U.S. Sixth Circuit Court of Appeals in Cincinnati. Former U.S. Secretary of War Newton D. Baker, a longtime Scripps lawyer who helped draw up the trust, defended Bob as the trustee and executor. It was an electrifying showdown. Millions of people in Ohio, California and the rest of the nation followed the courtroom confrontation. Other newspapers were delighted to put the Scripps family and company on the hot seat.

Ed was convinced that his mother was right and had a chance of winning the case. Hughes, a man of high principle, also believed in the case and told the family so. Ed, however, had a private foreboding. For years, the Scripps organization had great political clout in Cincinnati—not only because of the power of the *Post*, its newspaper there, but the fact that Scripps executives were leaders in the city's political, economic and social establishment. He also recalled words spoken by his mother years before—that some Scripps lawyers were capable of trying to buy judges. A considerable fortune was at stake—Josephine sued for $6 million—and neither the widow nor Ed trusted the Scripps leadership with one exception—Bob.

Mother and son had, from the beginning, felt awkward in suing Bob. He was their friend, confidant, and safe harbor. But Bob was the trustee and the key to a solution of their grievances. Now that

Josephine was appealing the lower court decision, she felt sure that Bob would not hide behind his company strategists and their lawyers. He was more than a friend; he was family. Uncle Bob knew that E.W. had put aside $6 million in securities for the day when he would meet his obligations to Jim. Bob would do the right thing by Josephine. He would not fight her appeal. Instead, Bob would turn over the $6 million to the widow and her children and wish them luck as family and news colleagues. They needed the money for their company to survive because, as Bob well knew, the papers which E.W. allowed Jim to buy so much stock in were his "dogs." All were struggling financially. None was sufficiently prosperous to carry the others. All of the papers were eventually to fall by the wayside.

Bob did not come out from behind his advisers, lawyers and his downtown desk. He shuffled papers and announced as the new E.W.: No!

If Bob had backed off and helped her, it is possible that Josephine's breakaway papers would have returned to the Scripps-Howard fold. But Bob's coldblooded defense and the bitter feeling that he had betrayed them caused the widow and Ed to decide that the split could not be healed. The dynasty would be divided as long as both would live.

In an astonishing early defense statement, Bob and attorney Baker claimed that E.W.'s annual profit and growth payments to Jim were "parental bounty"—gifts. Yet E.W. had written a letter to Jim on May 27, 1912:

"In making the proposal to divide with my sons half and half, the profits and increments of the business as they accrue under their management, I had no intention to make a gift. My sole object was but the just division of the profits to secure to the greatest possible extent, future interests of the concern.

"As from time to time I transfer to you certain stocks or other interests, I am only complying with the *agreements* (author's emphasis) already made and I am complying with these agreements solely for the purpose of securing for the future, better service . . ."

Each of the four payments made to Jim (a total of $815,000) was specifically designated by E.W. as a *partial* (author's emphasis) payment for services rendered. Hughes stated that E.W.'s requirement of "services rendered" eliminated the possibility of any gift. Josephine argued that E.W. had left an unpaid balance for her husband's services when the old man made out his trust. She was suing for precisely those funds.

Hughes declared that E.W. was under a "binding contractual obligation" to Jim regarding the performance of his work. Bob's lawyer insisted that E.W. had the power to terminate the business relationship at will. He did so in June of 1920. Hughes conceded the point but said that E.W. had a legal obligation to pay Jim for work performed before the agreement was broken by him.

Attorney Baker questioned whether E.W. and his sons ever intended to enter into a binding legal contract. He argued that the three had not expressly recognized or provided for the creation of legal obligations. It was purely a "business relationship." Jim himself did not want a written contract, although E.W. wrote and offered him one. The old man initialed every page of the contract. Hughes declared that the law, not the parties, fixes the requirements of a legal obligation. He said that the deliberate, serious promises of E.W. were enforceable irrespective of anyone's views regarding his legal liability.

The defense sought to avoid a letter which E.W. had written to his sons in May of 1912 in which he said: "Already the time has come when the relations between you and myself have changed from that of father and son, of chief and subordinate—of patron and dependent—to those of business partners."

In the same month, Scripps and his sons reinforced their 1911 agreement which stated that E.W. assumed an obligation once his sons' services for him were performed and he was bound to pay them at the rate fixed in the increment accord (an amount which E.W. considered fair).

Bob insisted that the statute of limitations had run out before Josephine had filed her case. He sought to have her appeal dismissed on the grounds that California law, under which Josephine

first filed the case, had two- and four-year periods for commence-
ment of a court action. Since E.W. had written his trust in 1923, the
California statutes had expired.

Josephine and Ed smiled at the duplicity of this stance. Everyone
in the family knew that E.W. claimed Ohio as his residence. Although California had long been his home and business office, E.W.
even took Bob to vote in Ohio. Through his political clout in the
governor's office and by setting up professional research chairs at
Miami University at Oxford, Ohio, E.W. arranged for Bob to be
appointed a trustee of the university in 1921, thus solidifying Bob
and himself as Ohio residents. That is why, even in the presence of
federal judges, Josephine and Ed feared the power of the E.W.
Scripps (holding) Company to fix the outcome of their appeal.

E.W.'s residency ruse was carried out to deny any claim that
Nackie might make against his will and trust under California law.
That state's community property statutes called for Nackie to re-
ceive half of her husband's estate.

Bob and his lawyers were attempting to use California to their
advantage in one area and deny it in another.

California statute-of-limitations law was actually on Josephine's
side. Any time that E.W. had spent outside the state could not be
counted against Josephine's court filing. Since the old man was at
sea most of the last three years of his life, the widow was on safe
ground. Bob pursued the California angle but failed.

This said much to Josephine and Ed about Bob's character. As the
appeal progressed, they slowly realized that their long, deep trust in
Bob had been misplaced. Both admitted that this confidence was
one of the biggest mistakes of their lives.

In a postscript to all this, attorney Baker attempted to bolster his
defense by saying that Josephine had "closed her own mouth" by
failing to bring suit against E.W. during his lifetime. Hughes retorted there was no basis for assuming that the widow ever realized
she would have to bring suit in Ohio—and even then her testimony
would be objected to on grounds that the California statute of
limitations had run out. Josephine's delay did not render her testimony inadmissible even under the Ohio statute.

Attorney Baker claimed that important oral and other evidence in the case may have been lost or destroyed. Hughes argued that there was too much uncontradicted evidence in the record to make such an assertion. Baker could prove no actual loss. Therefore, there was no evidence supporting the defense that E.W. changed his intention to pay Jim added bonuses as a result of his work.

Hughes presented various memos and other writings of E.W. to emphasize that the old man expected but wished to postpone litigation involving Jim and Bob's interests. E.W. was not arguing the rightness of Josephine's cause but, from the grave, he clearly supported her going to court. It was typical of him—sideswiping his own trustee. That was embarrassing for Bob and his defense.

Baker closed his case against Josephine on a note of irony. The defense claimed that Jim did not "fully or properly" perform the services required of him under the increment agreement with his father. Hughes then pointed out that Jim had managed and controlled more than thirty of the Scripps newspapers and, in addition, attended to his father's personal affairs. Baker asserted that Bob and Roy Howard had actually taken over Jim's job before his death and therefore his performance was not "full and proper." However, Josephine's claim was limited to the time which Jim served, not when the others assumed command. Finally, Hughes explained, the increment agreement between Jim and his father did not provide for Bob's entry.

Hughes closed his case in behalf of Josephine by quoting from E.W.'s writings shortly after Jim's death: "To give Josephine some idea of my attitude toward Jim, I briefly outlined my recent trip to the East during which I inspected a number of our offices. I told her that with one or two unimportant exceptions I found everywhere such a condition of affairs, such an organization of men and such a spirit of enterprise, good will and organization as to indicate that my son had been an exceedingly able administrator . . ."

The long battle between Jim and his father boiled down to this: Jim said it was unfair for E.W. to hold him responsible for the management of the business and, at the same time, require him to manage it according to the old man's judgment—not his own.

The fight was as old as biblical times. At least Josephine and Ed viewed it that way: a father and son went into business together. The father got old and asked the son to manage the business. The son, a man of more modern ways and times, wanted to make changes. The old man refused and turned to another son, who would follow his orders while accepting full responsibility for the future of the business. Meantime, the first son went to the elders of the tribe and asked for their opinion. The father had died, so the second son represented himself and the father. He claimed that his older brother was late in making any claim against the business, that he had not fully performed all the work, and—most importantly—there had never been any binding work agreement between the father and the first son. In biblical terms the two had never shaken hands on the deal. By the most charitable standards, Josephine and Ed believed, the second son did not have much of a case. That is the way that Josephine saw it until she died in 1959. And that is how Ed sees it today, sixty years after the trust was signed.

By a two-to-one vote on April 17, 1930, the U.S. Sixth Circuit Court of Appeals in Cincinnati rejected Josephine's appeal. In general terms, they ruled that an executed contract—not a business arrangement—was needed in order to create a binding legal obligation. The judges dismissed E.W.'s critical decision to take credit for the increment payments and profits on his federal income tax as part of a legal obligation or contract. They said it did not follow that either of the parties regarded E.W. as legally bound to pay his son's fifty percent of the annual profits and increment of his news enterprises despite promises to do so. The two judges added that no such obligation existed if he (E.W.) reserved to himself the ultimate right to determine the value of his sons' services and the amount of compensation that they should receive. The judges noted that four years elapsed between the last distribution to Jim and his death. Although Jim requested increment and annual profit payments to himself during that time, they argued that he never claimed them as a legal right.

The dissenting judge wrote that the agreement was a legal contract because compensation to Jim over a period of eight years had been recognized by both parties and was carried out. He said Jim's services were sufficiently identified. The judge denied Bob's claim that there was no way of measuring any possible due compensation with certainty. He said that was the "honest business judgment of the father." Since E.W. died before he could do this, that judgment was left to the courts. The judge explained that the parties appeared to have agreed on all aspects of their accord. If so, "a contract was complete."

The U.S. Supreme Court declined to hear an appeal by Josephine.

On March 2, 1938, Bob died of a hemorrhage in the throat caused by liver problems due to alcoholism. The last son of E.W. passed away as his father did—aboard a yacht in foreign waters. Bob was forty-two when he succumbed off the coast of Mexico. He was succeeded as trustee by his three sons—Charles, Bob and Ted. These were the three who voted to sell Miramar. Ted died of a heart attack in 1987 aboard a plane to Australia. Bob now runs a farm in Texas. Charles is chairman of the board of the E.W. Scripps Company.

Meantime, Jim's two sons—Ed and Jim—left the giant shadow of their grandfather and took another road. They created their own vision of the future.

4

A YOUNG MAN
WITH A MISSION

Ed Scripps was a young man with a mission. He would vindicate his father Jim and be worthy of the trust that his mother had placed in him. After spending six months at Southern California's Pomona College, which the Scripps family founded, Ed went to work as a cub reporter on Josephine's Spokane *Press*. He was sixteen years old. Ed's aim was to learn every facet of the newspaper business—from reporting to advertising, circulation, composing, and the complex printing machinery.

The year 1925 was not a time for men with a mission—unless it was a drink in your hand and a flapper on your arm. The country stood on its head in the midst of the Roaring Twenties. The national ambition was to make whoopee. Ed did not drink or smoke—or dance the Charleston. So the goodtime girls passed him by. He was, as the phrase went in those days, a strikeout king.

Ed Scripps at 16, shortly before he went to work as a cub
reporter at the Spokane
Press.

The editors and reporters on the *Press* soon learned that the new cub was an innocent who needed some of life's dirt behind his ears. Even though he was the owner's son, perhaps even because of it, they treated him like a batboy.

Ed's first assignment was to grow some beard (not easy for him at the time) and put on old clothes. Unemployment was rising in Spokane at the time and the paper wanted a better look at the problem. Ed was a big fellow, already well over six feet, weighing nearly 200 pounds. He was sent down to the local employment office to apply for a job—any job. The employment office had a job for him all right—on the loading dock of a manufacturing company lifting enough pipe every day for a sumo wrestler. The other newsmen chuckled as Ed dragged himself to the office after work each day to report in to the city editor. Mercifully, after four days, the editor was convinced the cub had enough information—and pipe—for his first feature story. The cub quit the loading dock the next day.

Ed's story was a surprise. He felt that every man on the dock had something special, even precious in him. Not money but character, will, hope. And most of all, they did not sidestep their problems. They met them head-on. Ed liked them. He saw himself that way. Ed recalls: "I had an exhilarating feeling putting that story together. Something ran up and down my spine. I had a feeling of empathy for the people involved. The experience stirred me. There could be few jobs like this. Reporting and writing were a very moving experience."

The young cub was sent to interview quack doctors, crazy murderers, and nutty old ladies. In emergencies, he was rushed out to help other reporters on big shootings, robberies, and fires. As the months passed, Ed couldn't shake the feeling that he was the paper's mascot.

Ed was very big in one department—carting home the paper's drunks. He would sometimes accompany the reporters and editors to a nearby saloon. He would learn a lot, listening to their talk about covering different stories. About the art of interviewing, listening instead of talking, being wary of practiced liars, and taking detailed notes. Ed loved every minute. This was life and human nature in the raw. He leaned back, sipped his homemade root beer, and smiled like a young Westerner riding a good horse.

As the evening wore on, some of the brethren were in no condition to walk home. At least not without the neighbors getting an eyeful. So, one by one, Ed would carry them to his old Dodge and hoist them into the back seat. In his early months at the paper, he had a difficult time finding their homes. Drunks do not always draw good road maps—or sputter the right directions. Ed recalls: "A wife would answer the doorbell and give me the evil eye: 'Oh, it's you again!' Not her husband who got drunk but me! I was the fall guy. I always wanted to get out of there in a hurry and said: 'Yes, it's me.' Sometimes she would stop me and ask: 'Where have you been?' What a question! As if I were responsible for her husband getting loaded! I had to make some excuse like: 'Oh, the poor fellow didn't have any dinner.' Or: 'It was an office get-together. He had to go.' It was a very uncomfortable chore but it was either that or not be accepted by the older reporters. I wanted to be accepted as much as anything in the world."

Despite the wrath of many wives, Ed felt fortunate: "None of them turned me away. Every one took her husband back. I had a perfect record!"

After a year on the Spokane *Press* and living in his first boarding house, Ed took several months off to read and study philosophy on his own. He felt this was the best way to develop his thinking process. But soon he returned to work as a young reporter on his mother's Seattle *Star*.

Ed's first assignment was unforgettable. Editor E.W. "Jorgy" Jorgenson sent him to interview Jean Harlow. The actress was the Marilyn Monroe of her day—slinky, sexy and, at times, sizzling.

Harlow was in Seattle publicizing a new movie and staying at a

The staff of the Seattle *Star*, where young Ed's first assignment was to interview Jean Harlow. From left: standing: H.E. Marshall, G. Donohue, Jim Scripps, A. Shannon, F. Taylor, D. Andrews; seated: H.W. Parish, A.J. Ritchie, F.W. Webster, B. Hoon, E. Grenfell.

downtown hotel. She agreed to be interviewed in her suite. Ed knocked on her door and said he was the reporter from the *Star*. Harlow opened the door—stark naked.

Ed was cross-eyed with surprise. He began to stutter. Harlow ordered him in and closed the door. She walked to a couch, sat, and draped one leg over the other. That was her only concession to modesty. Her bare breasts were still on parade. The actress, perhaps thinking of lunch, was anxious to get the interview started and over.

Ed tried to stop his stuttering. He was not a cub anymore. This was the big time and he was man enough for it. But something was wrong with her hair. He noted that it was different shades of blonde at various parts of her head. It was platinum on the left, straw-colored on the right with a mix in the middle.

Harlow lit a cigarette. The smoke billowed in front of her face and the rise and fall of her chest. Ed had to get hold of himself. He must stop blushing and be dignified.

Harlow hit all of his questions out of the park. Her movie was a great drama. Clark Gable was an adorable man. After her publicity tour, she was rushing back to Hollywood for an adventure film. She could furnish the *Star* with studio photos of herself on the latest film set. She was wearing less. There were so many different clothes to wear in a film and so much makeup. She preferred natural beauty. Harlow had finished her cigarette. She ground it into a silver ash tray and explained she didn't have much more time. There was a schedule to meet. Ed could see her face and nipples clearly once more. Harlow walked to a piano in the middle of her suite. Ed began to stutter again softly to himself: Was she going to play or sing? Or just show off her magnificent bare behind and legs? Harlow pulled several photos from a studio publicity kit and handed them to Ed. She was already walking to the door. Ed rose and followed her. For the first time, he noticed she was wearing shoes—silver-colored high heels. Before he knew it, Ed was out in the hallway and Harlow had closed her door. He stood limp in the hallway. Something told him that she was looking out the door's peephole, laughing. That's the way he remembered her—with an amused smile on her face.

Ed returned to tell Jorgy of the interview. He feared the editor would never believe him. But Jorgy did and milked every detail out of the embarrassed Ed as the listening staff tittered and then broke out in loud guffaws.

Sally Rand, the fan dancer, also came to Seattle. Ed was a natural to interview her. Jorgy assigned him to the story. Sally was completely dressed, so she didn't bring her fan. One had to pay to see Sally without her colorful clothes. Ed told Jorgy that she was a nice, polite lady. The reporters broke into wild laughter again. Ed figured Gypsy Rose Lee could not be far behind. The stripper never showed during Ed's residence in Seattle, but he met her at a party years later. Ed said she was nice, too. And Gypsy thought he was a gentleman.

Aimee Semple McPherson, the evangelist, came to town but Ed was never convinced she was a lady. Jorgy assigned Ed to attend some of her revival meetings and eventually interview her. This time he was shocked.

The dynamic preacher who seemed to flash lightning bolts when she spoke, would first warm up the congregation with lively hymns and the thunder of her words. Some in the audience would go limp while others fainted. At this time, Aimee invited the ill and lame to come up on the stage with their bandages and crutches. She would wave her hand over their heads in what seemed to be a mystical motion. The healed would throw off their bandages and crutches in what seemed to be a flood of ecstasy. They walked back to their seats among a heavenly chorus of hallelujahs and amens.

Collection boxes weren't used because Aimee didn't want to hear any change. Instead, long lines of thin rope with clothespins were stretched across the pews. The faithful were expected to pin at least a dollar bill to the line. Ed noticed that some poor folk would put as much as a ten-dollar bill on the line. He was horrified. The young reporter considered Aimee an evangelical hustler.

Ed later interviewed Aimee in her temporary office. She may have sensed his antagonism because she demanded he come up with a check before she would continue the interview. He didn't and Aimee said Amen. Ed was shown the door—to the fires of unbelievers.

Ed Scripps canoeing on Lake Washington, circa 1911.

There was one more fire to cover before Ed left the *Star*'s reporting staff. The fire of love—the paper's advice-to-the-lovelorn column. The woman who wrote it was going on vacation. Jorgy told Ed
that he was the only one available and couldn't say no. Besides, Jorgy
told Ed, he was young and could make the column young at heart.

It was all heartache. Ed never knew there were so many cheating
husbands in the world, so many amorous women who wondered
whether their lovers would really marry them, the battered wife,
and the lazy bum with four kids who wouldn't get a job. Ed recalls
the first letter that he answered from a reader. Her husband was
concealing a hot office romance. What should she do?

Here he was, not yet twenty-one, single and without even a steady
girl. In fact, dates were few and far between. Ed was too reserved

and, when he did get on the dance floor, he had too many feet. He
had taken up boxing and cooking. He had to learn to cook. He had
an apartment now. It was too expensive to eat out. And he had to get
more exercise than pounding a typewriter. He had to work out his
frustrations and disappointments on the punching bag.

Ed sat for a couple of hours tossing his pencil in the air. The
answer wasn't in an abstract definition of gravity. This was stomach-
wrenching guts, hot-blooded anger, and perhaps the woman was
even suicidal. Ed studied her letter again. No, she didn't write like
someone about to hang herself. But she needed advice, an expert,
the wisdom of the ages.

Ed sat there for three hours without typing a word. He was lucky
that Alice, or whatever her name was, had left him the cushion of a
couple of columns. Some whiz-bang authority he was. Well, he never
claimed to be an expert. Who did Jorgy think he was anyway? Hell,
he didn't know any more about love than the switchboard operator.
And secretly, she might know a lot more.

He finally began to peck out a reply on the typewriter. First, these

Ed and other executives at the Portland *News-Telegram*.

problems were as old as Eve. She must be calm, steady, possessed. No, that was the wrong word. He crossed out "possessed." She was already possessed. She should not march down to her husband's office. Confrontation was no answer. Embarrassment never solved anything. She should write the woman a letter. It should say that she knew about the romance and, if it wasn't over immediately, she planned to make it public. If the woman told a single person about her letter, including her husband, she would also go public. In any event, she was pregnant again. If for no other reason than the innocent, unborn child, the woman must leave its father immediately. Well, it might be a bit of a fib since the reader's letter only hinted she might be expecting. But what a smash answer! What a knockout punch! Oops, he was not on the sports page. Maybe he was boxing too much. What a good, reasonable bit of advice. That was real lovelorn wisdom.

Ed was never comfortable in the lovelorn job. There was always a small mountain of letters on the desk. He was constantly re-

Josephine L. Scripps, Ed's sister, and a friend, circa 1928.

minded of his fallibility. He could blow it all with one dumb reply. The next letter said—Oh, Lord—the woman was pregnant with no husband.

For two weeks, Ed sweated blood and tears. He was becoming a nervous wreck. When the regular columnist returned to the office, he wanted to kiss her. He knew that would never do, so he shook her hand—and shook and shook. The startled woman was ready to demand that Ed unleash her except that he had such a pleased smile on his face. He finally walked off bowing, smiling, and looking ever so relieved.

After his lovelorn imprisonment and several years as a reporter, Ed was ready for a new challenge. The circulation department is the newspaper's front line. From a late paper to a nondelivered copy, from a rain-soaked edition to a missing comics or sports section, the customer is furious—and always right, even when he's wrong.

The *Star* had nearly fifty circulation districts staffed by young part-time managers. Each manager had about forty carriers under him. An executive directed the operation with a staff at the paper's headquarters. He was also responsible for delivery trucks, sales racks and collection money. Mr. Donoghue—that's how he preferred to be addressed—ran this operation.

It was a job with a thousand headaches a day—from late papers after a press breakdown, to rain, missing managers and dozens of carriers out with the flu. Ed suffered the irate telephone calls and other anguish with the staff. He concluded that publishing and delivering a newspaper really was a daily miracle.

In the midst of this madness, Donoghue was the soul of tranquility. He had a way of turning away trouble, including wrathful subscribers. Ed began studying the master. He remembers a typical customer:

"This large woman came into the office to pay her bill. But before she paid, the woman slammed down a rain-soaked paper on the counter and said she wanted to see the boss. Donoghue no sooner arrived than she shouted:

" 'Look at this! This is the way my paper was delivered. And I am supposed to pay for *this*!'

"Donoghue had a regular routine. He would look the woman square in the eyes, nod deferentially to her, and say:

" 'Madame, you are right! You are absolutely right!'

"He would call over his top circulation manager and say: 'This happened in your district. Will you explain to this lady why her newspaper was not delivered to her doorknob as it should have been. It was soaked like *this* when she got it.' "

Donoghue would invariably pause to let his seriousness soak in— not to his manager but into the woman's mind. When he resumed speaking, his voice was irate:

" 'Now I warned you about this before, several times, in fact. I told you that if this happened again you were going to be fired. I'm sorry to have to tell you now that you're . . .' "

It never failed. The customer would always interrupt at this point. No one wanted to see anyone fired over one lousy paper delivery. The customer would say:

" 'Oh, don't do that! He won't let it happen again. Maybe it was really someone else's fault. Let's forget it this time.' "

Donoghue would make sure he collected from the customer before he shook his or her hand. He would say:

"If it happens again, come to see me. I'll make it right!"

He did, in his own way. Donoghue always called those responsible for a foulup. He explained the complaint and calmly asked the offender to be more careful.

Ed Scripps never forgot Donoghue. To this day, he says: "A mild answer turneth away wrath."

Ed moved to advertising. The *Star* manager there had a slightly different approach. A woman had placed an ad in the paper and it was an unreadable mess. A staff member was summoned as the woman impatiently waited for justice. The staffer was told:

"Smith, your ad has this lady's house upside down. Her chimney is at the bottom and welcome mat at the top. I can't figure out if this is a jungle gym ad or a house for sale. Smith, I've told you before that this kind of work could bring down the ax on you. What do you have to say?"

The customer always halted the ax. Smith apologized to the woman. He would do it right. And, the manager exclaimed, so would the *Star*. This and the next ad that she put in the paper would be free. The *Star* had made a friend for life.

Josephine's newspapers hired more women than any of their competition. Ed found that women were particularly good at soliciting classified advertising because of their "sweeter, more unruffled attitude." Another reason was, the widow's papers were the second, third and fourth publications in their markets and could not offer top salaries. They earned a profit but it was a constant struggle.

Ed kept growing and at the age of twenty he was six feet four and one-half inches tall, weighing nearly 220 pounds. He would climb to 250 pounds. Ed continued his childhood sports—riding horses, boating and swimming—but felt they didn't offer enough exercise. He took up body building and weights and continued to box, getting into the ring with some of the pros who hung around the Seattle Athletic Club. He had a powerhouse left hook.

Ed continued his news training and on April 10, 1929, his mother wrote to him: "You have established a very high reputation for yourself among the old men of the Scripps-Howard as well as the Scripps-Canfield concern. I know you rather well, as I have been studying you, and I am willing to bet our whole estate that you will go through life a credit to yourself and will also be a substantial and reliable guide and leaning post to those less fortunate about new ideas and clear thinking . . ."

Ed's brother Jim joined the financial staff at the company's Seattle headquarters. Jim was a math whiz and enjoyed that type of work. On August 13, 1929, Josephine wrote to her sons: "It is a great comfort to me that you boys are learning the business real fast."

In 1931 New York governor Franklin D. Roosevelt came to Seattle in his quest for the Democratic presidential nomination. Ed interviewed him. FDR said that, if elected, he would develop the territory of Alaska, especially its vast coal fields. This was big news since it would mean a major economic lift for the state of Washington. Ed, a political independent, was impressed with Roosevelt's idealism.

He believed that this was an honest man who would work for the benefit of the entire country, and he was delighted when FDR was elected.

Once in the White House, Ed concluded that Roosevelt forgot about Alaska and other promises. About two years after FDR assumed office, he took the United States off the gold standard and made it illegal to possess gold. This came soon after Ed had taken his life's savings, some $400,000, out of government bonds and bought gold as an investment.

Ed was deeply troubled. The discipline of the gold standard was the country's best hedge against inflation. The need to pay out solid gold when investors demanded their money made bankers much less careless with what they did with investments. Gold also improved ethics in the nation's credit markets.

Ed's new and troubling judgment of Roosevelt gave way to horror. He learned that, prior to his announcement on gold, FDR advised J. Pierpont Morgan of what he was about to do. The New York banker owned a fortune in gold and quickly found a loophole to keep

Scripps-Canfield Conference, June 1930.

his holdings. A brief clause in the ruling made an exception for gold on foreign consignment. Morgan had his gold on ships to Europe before Roosevelt's announcement was made. Ed sold his gold back to the federal government at a large loss. He kept one ten-dollar gold piece as a reminder of what he considered FDR's betrayal.

Gold stood for only half of Ed's anger. He concluded that FDR, instead of seeking a genuine balance of views on the U.S. Supreme Court, was packing it with liberal Democrats. No president in U.S. history had ever demeaned juridical fairness or the balance of the high court in such blatant fashion.

Ed still carries that ten-dollar gold piece. It's a reminder of not only FDR's duplicity but the fickleness of political ethics. The coin also serves as a caution to Ed himself—to be a man of integrity with no false promises.

Ed's best friend in Seattle was Joshua "Josh" Green. Both were intelligent, single, athletic and ambitious. The friendship was to influence much of Ed's financial life. The young man's father—another Josh—was the owner of Seattle's People's Bank. Ed's phone

Ed Scripps hunting with friends in the Pacific Northwest. On the far right is Josh Green, his best friend in Seattle.

at the *Star* rang one morning. It was Josh, Sr. Could Ed do him a favor? He wanted to meet the family that owned the H.F. Alexander Steamship Line. The line made regular calls at West Coast ports from San Diego to Vancouver. Ed was flattered that Josh, Sr., thought he knew the Alexanders but he did not. Never mind, the banker said, you have the right credentials to get to know them. He would tell Ed how to do it.

Ed was hesitant. Why did Mr. Green want to know the Alexanders? Ornamental tile, Josh, Sr., said. Tile? Ed asked. Yes, his friend's father said, he wanted the Alexanders' tile company account in his bank.

This was a bit much and Ed took a deep breath. Mr. Green explained that Alexander franchises selling specially colored tile were sweeping the state of Washington and other parts of the West. It was a new, growing company with considerable potential. He would go out and ride a horse—except that he didn't know how—to get the business. Rather, Ed and young Josh would saddle up.

What does that mean? Ed asked. Play polo, Josh, Sr., replied. Polo? Ed inquired. Yes, Mr. Green said, you own some of those fancy outfits in which people play polo and your family has several horses. Ed said that was correct. Well, Ed could outfit himself and Josh, Jr., with riding clothes and boots and go meet the Alexanders, father and son, on the polo field. The banker had already scouted them there. Did Josh, Jr., play polo? No, the father said, but Ed could teach him the rules in one afternoon. Josh was a fair rider.

How and where were they to meet the Alexanders? With Ed playing polo with Josh, Jr., at a certain field until the Alexanders showed up, the father explained. Ed would introduce himself and Josh to the Alexanders. Just like that? Ed questioned. Just like that, the banker responded.

Ed and young Josh met the Alexanders a few weeks later. The father got the ornamental tile account and never forgot it. As long as he lived, the banker acted as a friendly financial counselor to Ed and his family. His bank not only helped finance newspaper deals when Ed needed the money, but acted as an intermediary when they sought loans from others.

In the course of his life when anyone asked: Polo anyone? Ed had his boots and saddle ready.

Josephine's five breakaway newspapers plus three new additions were incorporated in 1931 into the Scripps League of Newspapers, Inc. In five earlier years, from 1926 to 1931, Josephine bought three small newspapers on the advice of Milton McRae. Two were located in Utah, at Provo and Logan, while the third was at Coeur d'Alene, Idaho. At twenty-one Ed became the league's president and board chairman and assumed full command of the eight papers, and his brother Jim was promoted to become a top financial executive.

Several months before the incorporation, Ed began thinking about distinguishing the new organization from Scripps-Howard. The Scripps-Howard papers carried a lighthouse as a logo with the words: "Give light and the people will find their own way." He decided to use the torch of the Statue of Liberty as the Scripps League symbol. It would proclaim freedom throughout the country.

However, no artist was able to draw a torch to Ed's satisfaction. As he now recalls: "A lot of them looked like an artichoke being held out by the goddess of liberty."

It took a year and scores of drawings before the torch finally appeared in the three Scripps League papers. To Ed, his mother and brother, it privately symbolized their freedom from Scripps-Howard and aspirations for the future. Today, because of their editorial independence, Scripps League papers are free to use the torch or not. Some do not.

The Depression knocked the country down but most newspapers, including the Scripps League, did relatively well. Advertising continued high because, to make money in the very competitive marketplace, businesses were forced to rely on newspaper ads.

In 1933 Ed married Mary Oldham, a young woman from a fine Seattle family. They had three children, two daughters and a son. One daughter, Sheila, died young of cancer. The second, Stephanie, has made a career with the U.S. Army. The son, E.W. Scripps III, is an executive with the Scripps League of Newspapers. The couple drifted apart and separated on amicable terms, divorcing in 1948 after fifteen years of marriage. Oldham, who has not remarried, still lives in Seattle on a substantial income of her own. Ed never discusses his former wife.

Meantime, Josephine wanted Ed to broaden his education. She promised to pay her son $100 every time he read a serious book. Ed jumped at the chance and read thirty books in less than two years. He banked $3,000 for the proverbial rainy day. One of those books was philosopher Oswald Spengler's *The Decline of the West*, which Ed still rereads today. That and other works made him a lifetime student of philosophy and history.

Ed's mother returned to live with her daughter Josephine at Fanita Ranch, and Ed now ran the organization totally. The papers continued profitable but the organization remained stagnant from 1935 until after the war. Ed was uncomfortable with the market positions of the breakaway newspapers. They were being squeezed by larger, more profitable papers in areas that would not eventually support their current three or four publications. Ed and Jim were concerned about the future.

In the mid-1930s, Ed started a new business with a Seattle mechanic by the name of Pearson. They made specialized parts for ships under a subcontract agreement. The two also constructed a special spiral to adjust the wing flaps of planes. When World War II began, the U.S. Navy needed these specialized bolts and other parts for military landing ships and the U.S. Air Force wanted the adjusters for their wing flaps. Ed's work was ruled essential to the nation's military buildup and he was deferred from the draft. The company made cement mixers after the war. It was a marginal operation because of stiff competition from larger companies. The firm eventually went out of business, but Ed never lost his love of mechanics.

After the war, despite good times across most of the economy, newspaper advertising nose-dived. Slowly, one by one, Ed began to sell or fold all of the breakaway papers. He also sold three radio stations that the family had purchased. Ed had made one of the most crucial decisions of his career—to place the league's future in small exclusive markets with greater growth potential. These would be markets similar to those where Josephine had earlier bought papers in Utah and Idaho. He would use the income from the sale of the larger newspaper, radio and other properties as a base to build a completely new organization. Ed did not accept the Scripps-Howard view that bigger was better economically or that central headquarters should dominate local editorial and financial judgment. He was to pull a page from E.W.'s book and stress local independence.

Ed was working hard but he was lonely. His brother Jim had married an attractive young woman, Marion Bates, from a well-established Seattle family. They were having children and were very happy.

In 1949 the George De Vries family, which was in the California dairy business, suggested to Ed that he meet a young lady friend of theirs. Her name was Betty Jeanne Knight McDonnell. Her father was a California business executive.

The two met under the clock in the lobby of San Francisco's St. Francis Hotel. Ed was stunned. She was very young—twenty-three. He was forty. She was a slim, beautiful blonde. He was tall, athletic and handsome—but no movie star. She was Hollywood material. Hal Roach, the producer, had already offered her a film contract but her father turned it down. There was a catch to this magical moment—her mother accompanied Betty.

The three had lunch at the St. Francis. Ed couldn't take his eyes off the young woman. He couldn't believe his luck—beauty, personality, and brains. It was too good to be true. There was only one problem: She had to leave mother at home.

The friendship lengthened into weeks and months. Candlelight dinners, the symphony, boating. Betty looked better to Ed every week. Her mother tended to her knitting at home. His luck was holding.

Betty's family was well known in the Bay area. Her mother Eleanor Knight was the daughter of a French father from the Avignon area and a Belgian mother, the daughter of Sir François Prospère Williame of Florenville. The two had emigrated to the United States and eventually settled in San Francisco. Betty's father's family had come from England in 1676. Some of the family later settled in West Virginia where the family had substantial land holdings and business interests. This is where Betty's father, Cecil Howard Knight, grew up. Betty was born in Denver but her father was transferred by his firm to Rapid City, South Dakota, and later to San Francisco. Betty was reared in the Bay area—in San Francisco and nearby Burlingame and Hillsboro. She was a very active youngster, taking part in ballet, piano, theater, debating, tennis and other sports. Betty attended San Mateo College and Stanford University for a few months but dropped out in 1944 to marry her high school sweetheart, Barry L. McDonnell, Jr. After Barry returned from service with the Coast Guard in the South Pacific, he joined his family's electrical contracting firm in San Francisco. They had a son, Barry, but discovered that they no longer had much in common and separated in 1948, divorcing two years later.

Ed was absolutely certain that he was in love about four months after meeting Betty. The convincer was when he ran out of gas on the Nevada desert. Nobody, he told himself, would run out of gas in the torrid desert miles from nowhere unless he were lovestruck or crazy. Ed gave himself the benefit of the doubt and said it must be love. And he finally managed to find a gas station.

One evening, Ed met Betty at a San Mateo restaurant and, after dinner, pulled out a small jeweler's box when the two got in his car. He opened the box, showed her a large diamond, explained it was his mother's engagement ring, and said nothing. The next move was up to her. Betty put on the ring; it was somewhat loose but she accepted without a pause. That was the happiest moment of Ed's life.

Early in the engagement, Ed took Betty to meet the Scripps clan at a family gathering in La Jolla. The bride-to-be felt that most of the Scrippses seemed unusually reserved during the introductions. The only woman who showed her deference and genuine warmth

Ed and Betty Scripps at their engagement party at her parents' home in Hillsborough, California.

was Ed's mother. As Ed later learned, most of the family regarded the young filly as too beautiful and elegant to be a Scripps. Betty felt not only cold-shouldered but scared by the encounter. The meeting did not sit comfortably with the Scripps family's Latin motto: *Aspiciens in Futurum*—Looking to the Future.

Ed was in a hurry. He wanted to get married at once. However, Betty's divorce would not be final for seven months. Ed consulted Sammy Hahn, the Los Angeles attorney representing the Scripps League papers. Hahn suggested the two marry in Cuernavaca, Mexico. Betty consulted her parents. Her mother said no—no, no, no. Ed was insistent. Betty returned to her mother. Mrs. Knight finally said: It's up to you. Ed and Betty flew to Cuernavaca a few days later.

"It was very romantic," Betty now remembers. "Ed bought me a white hand-made Mexican wedding dress with hand-embroidered flowers. I still have it. We stopped at a jewelry store and he got me a little gold filagreed amethyst cross on a gold chain for my neck. The afternoon ceremony was held in the side chapel of a small church. A civil magistrate officiated. The driver, whom we had hired at the airport, and his wife were witnesses. Ed and I were both teary-eyed. The driver and his wife kept raining rice on us. The ceremony was in Spanish. After we had taken our vows, one set of documents was placed in what appeared to be an archives section of the chapel. We received the other set."

The driver drove the newlyweds to Cuernavaca's largest hotel. The manager greeted them and immediately offered cocktails in celebration. A leisurely dinner followed. When the two awoke the following morning, they decided to go swimming and put on their swim suits. The pool had no water. A bellman announced:

"The pool will open in two years."

With that, the newlyweds returned to the West Coast. Betty's California divorce was not yet final, so they lived at Lake Tahoe, Nevada, until it was completed. Mr. and Mrs. Knight wanted a religious ceremony at their home in Hillsboro. So, on January 31, 1950, the day that Betty's divorce became final, the two were wed a second time by a Presbyterian minister. Only family and a few close friends were invited. The couple moved briefly into the Knights' Hillsboro home, which was designed by Frank Lloyd Wright student Richard Neutra. It was a beautiful three-story place, built of stone and glass, featuring an entire wall fresco by Sotomeyer, the protégé of Diego Rivera. The painting was a hunting scene located near the large bar. Betty's father Howard often told guests that, when the tiger turned its head, you had too much to drink. The room overlooked the lawn and canyon beyond. Today the estate is one of two Hillsboro homes listed in the National Register of outstanding architecture in the United States. The other is the Carolands. Betty and Ed then moved to nearby Atherton where Ed had been building a place for them on five acres. Then they entrained for New York—Betty's wide-eyed first visit—and took the *Queen Mary* to England for a honeymoon in Europe. The winter voyage was rough. While seated for dinner at the

Ed and Betty on their honeymoon aboard the *Queen Mary*.

captain's table, Betty announced that she needed to stretch out on the dining room floor. It was seasickness—not cocktails. Rather than witness the distress from that angle, the captain personally walked off the queasiness with Betty on deck.

Ed took her to most of the sights in London, Paris, and Rome. Betty made one mistake. She had a martini with a woman reporter at the bar of the Crillon Hotel. When the world stopped spinning, she woke up in bed. Ed asked dutifully:

"Have you had a nice rest?"

"Wonderful," Betty said. "Just wonderful. Where are we?"

"Paris," he replied.

If she didn't know where she was, Betty knew it was time to go home. The honeymooners returned to California and Ed returned to work. He moved the League's headquarters from Seattle to San Mateo, near Atherton. In the months ahead, Ed held various receptions and dinners to introduce his wife to most of the Scripps family. Their reception of Betty remained the same—cold. Ed recalls:

"Many of the Scripps women were not distinguished by beauty. Betty's youth, energy, and attractiveness was a shock to them. So was her quick intelligence. I'm sorry to say that I believe there was an almost instinctive jealousy on the part of the Scripps women."

Betty was someone in her own right—a Daughter of the American Revolution and a member of the Colonial Dames of America—and she and Ed were about to launch their own revolution.

5

A NEW VISION

As the 1950s began, the United States was on top of the world. All of Europe and many other nations around the globe were still rebuilding from World War II. The economic, political and social power of America—including its military might—was at its zenith. U.S. business was booming. Big was beautiful. Bigger was best.

Many large American newspapers, however, had been in the doldrums since the end of the war. Radio had taken a big slice of their advertising. More cars had put millions of commuters behind the wheel, instead of behind the daily paper. Migration from big cities to the suburbs was creating new newspaper costs and delivery problems. The circulation of afternoon newspapers had begun to slide. Television was just around the corner and even its makeshift news programs made the entire newspaper industry uncomfortable.

After buying his fourth small daily paper in 1949, The Dalles

Three young men in the news business, from the left: Jim Scripps, his cousin John P. Scripps and brother Ed.

(Oregon) *Chronicle*, Ed Scripps had about $100,000 left in savings plus several hundred thousand more from the sale of his mother's breakaway papers.

Ed then made a crucial decision which he was to stand by for the next forty years: Think small town. Rather than buy secondary papers in large markets, he would purchase the only paper in small towns. A small town meant a population of under 100,000—often much below that. Ed's four current publications fit his strategy—the Provo *Daily Herald* and Logan *Herald* in Utah, the Coeur d'Alene *Press* and The Dalles *Chronicle*. Ed's brother Jim joined as his partner and performed most of the office financial work. Unlike their father Jim and his brother Bob, the two got along well.

Ed and Betty Scripps were thinking big financially—not small—to buy and own twenty newspapers across the country. They would have to drive the highways and byways of state after state as they sized up papers to purchase. In the old days, this was no problem for Ed. He hopped on his motorcycle and was in business. Now there was a problem. Ed had taken Betty on a motorcycle ride after they were married. With Betty holding on for life and limb, dressed in slacks, a skirt and sweater, Ed raced another couple down the main drag near their home in Atherton. She has never gotten on a motorcycle since.

Ed thought long and hard. Finally, with heavy heart, he made his decision. His bride would ride comfortably in a car. They drove to Provo, Logan and Coeur d'Alene so Betty could get a better idea of how newspapers functioned. They could also assess the prospects for the papers and chart a clearer course for the future. Ed recalls:

"I had three other purposes: To get into a different part of journalism than the large papers of Scripps-Howard. Small-town newspapering appealed to me. I was more of a country person than a city fellow. My financial and circulation figures showed that small towns were the wave of the future.

"Second, I wanted my life to be of service. This was a civic and religious conviction that came from my mother and father. I was always attracted to communities with spiritual values. Good schools and churches, a good work ethic, a wholesome environment. I always looked for these in buying a paper because they were signs that the community would do well. In return, my aim was to be of genuine service to that community. To help make it a better place to live.

"Finally, my own personal identity became very important. Maybe that's why I rode a motorcycle. People who ride motorcycles are making a personal statement about individual freedom. It became a personal affront when some executive from Scripps-Howard would say to me: 'E.W. wouldn't have done it that way.' I didn't want to ride on E.W.'s coattails like the Scripps-Howard crowd. I wanted to rise or fall on my own—Ed Scripps, not E.W., as much as I respected him."

With Jim minding the California office, Ed and Betty headed for Utah. Both felt that their family break with Scripps-Howard was final. They were now headed in a completely different direction. Betty recalls:

"The *Herald* was in a tiny building on a side street. The structure

The Provo *Herald* building, which Betty saw for the first time on her honeymoon.

was leaning to the right. A flat sign hung from the building. Ed beamed: 'This is the Provo paper.' All I could reply was: 'Oh.' "

The two visited with the *Herald* staff and drove to Logan. Betty remembers:

"Logan also had a small paper in a tiny building. Ed said: 'This is the Logan *Herald*.' I said: 'Oh.' We searched for a place to sleep that night. There was a little old hotel up the street, so we took a room. The cubicle had an iron-sided brass bed. A flash of red-and-white color splashed across the bedspread from the neon sign at a movie house across the street. Ed, forever the optimist, said: 'You're really going to like it here.' I replied: 'Oh.'

"He took me to the Bluebird Cafe for dinner. Dinner was forgettable but the homemade chocolate chip ice cream was wonderful. In later years, whenever we went to Logan, I always insisted that we eat at the Bluebird so we could have chocolate chip.

"We visited with the Logan staff and headed for Coeur d'Alene. Ed and Burl Hagadone, a real go-getter, were partners in the *Press* there. Coeur d'Alene is, of course, a very beautiful place with its lake and the nearby mountains. So I expected a fairly new operation. Ed said: 'This is the Coeur d'Alene paper.' It was an old grocery store converted to a newspaper plant. I said: 'Oh.'

"The total circulation of the three papers was about 15,000. Yet Ed was so optimistic, so enthusiastic. He kept telling me that he could see down the road and these papers were going to grow and be big in their communities. But it all looked about the same to me—a long, narrow, difficult road for us. But I said: 'Oh, Ed, it's wonderful!' "

The newlyweds drove to Salt Lake City, where they took a suite in the large, modern Hotel Utah. Betty recalled that a letter waited for

The presses of the Coeur d'Alene *Press*, one of the first papers Ed and Betty visited on their honeymoon.

Ed. He read it when they got to their room and put the letter in his pocket. Betty asked him whom the note was from. He said it wasn't important. She insisted: "Look, dear, we're married now. We share our lives. Who wrote you the letter?"

He handed the note to Betty. It was from an old girlfriend who lived in Salt Lake. She had heard that Ed was staying at the hotel. The young lady said she understood Ed was engaged and about to marry a wealthy woman with a houseful of kids. She added: "I guess you're marrying her for monetary reasons . . ." Betty burst out laughing. Yes, all her multimillions! The old flame concluded that she wasn't doing so well and would appreciate it if Ed would spread his newfound wealth around, particularly in her direction. Ed blushed but Betty laughed. She told Ed that it was a good idea for her to come on these trips. She would protect him from his old flames and, in a pinch, lend him a few bucks.

Ed and Betty were to buy more newspapers in the 1950s—the *Arizona Daily Sun* in Flagstaff, and the Hanford (California) *Sentinel*, four papers in Idaho and two in Montana. He would make a "hit list"—hit the road, not a shooting spree—of about twenty potential purchases. Ed and Betty would then gas up their car and drive thousands of miles in every region of the country. Before they started off, Ed would fly to New York and visit *Editor & Publisher* the newspaperman's bible. He cross-checked *E&P* population and retail sales trends of independent newspapers for a decade against those of the U.S. Census Bureau. He always studied the sources of all *E&P* figures and discussed findings with the staff responsible for the numbers.

Ed and Betty would then drive to the prospective newspaper, where he would examine its financial books over a ten-year period, if possible. Ed would then study the competing paper, if there was one. He would next start smelling. In the case of Provo, it was the steel being made. At Logan, the rich smell of farmland. In Coeur d'Alene, the good smell of a clean, vibrant environment. If there was a dull, vapid smell in any town, Ed would pass up the paper.

He also had a habit of going to supermarket parking lots and studying the license plates. Ed would count the percentage of those plates that originated in nearby counties. That meant the advertising base was expansive and could be extended. This was also a double-check against the paper's own figures on retail sales. He also studied crime rates and church attendance. If crime was high and churchgoing was low, that could tilt against his purchase.

There was, of course, much more to consider—the paper's presses and plant, other mechanics, executive ability, staff morale, loan financing and, especially, growth potential. Ed looked at eventual profit as E.W. had: an annual fifteen percent cash divisible net profit—not book profit. Ed and Betty sometimes visited a dozen papers before they decided to buy one. Josh Green was always ready to help in financing, but Ed often didn't need his assistance. The name of Scripps was a big door-opener at many banks. Ed thanked E.W. for some of that but he also had a good reputation as a businessman. As a result, he bought many papers with only ten percent down.

Ed kept extensive files on the papers he purchased and those he chose not to buy. They not only reminded him of his evaluation processes but reasons for returning to look at the paper again.

Ed had a rule which other newspaper owners respected and admired. He never played one owner off against another to haggle a paper's price down. Ed says:

"I considered that unethical and never did it in my life. I've always believed in paying a fair price for a property. My colleagues knew that and were aware that I was not going to dicker much. It saved both of us a lot of time and trouble. I always looked less at the paper's price than its potential expansion."

The Provo *Daily Herald* was typical of what Ed looked and hoped for in a newspaper. Although the newspaper was purchased by his mother in 1926, it represented the best of his thinking and even had two historical ties to his grandfather. The paper was founded in 1873, the year when E.W. was starting to learn the newspaper business on the Detroit *Evening News*. It was then the Provo *Daily Times*. At the time, the pioneer town had a population of 2,500. The *Times* was founded by a Civil War veteran, Robert G. Sleater, and three partners. The paper also was bought the same year that E.W.

The staff of the Provo *Herald* around the time that Josephine Stedem Scripps acquired it in 1926.

died. Ed viewed the coincidental timing as a passing of the torch from his grandfather to his parents.

Provo was founded in 1849, less than two years after the Mormons arrived in the Valley of the Great Salt Lake. It is about forty-five miles south of Salt Lake City in a valley dominated by the Wasatch Mountains and Utah Lake, a large basin of fresh water that drains northward into the Great Salt Lake. Brigham Young University is the intellectual and cultural center of the city. Provo and its sister city, Orem, have the highest concentration of Mormons in the world—more than ninety-five percent of their population are members of the Church of Jesus Christ of Latter-day Saints. Betty liked Provo, since some members of her father's family had been Mormons.

The *Herald* is the Scripps League flagship newspaper, with a daily circulation of nearly 32,000 copies. Today the market area of Provo-Orem has a population of more than 100,000.

Provo has always been a Mormon community. Its struggle against the intrusion of the federal government, as well as persecution that followed its members from Ohio, Missouri and Illinois, has long been recounted on the pages of the *Herald*.

Shortly after the Scrippses bought the *Herald*, two historic events occurred—the 1928 presidential battle between Republican Herbert Hoover and Democrat Al Smith. The race became embroiled in religion because Smith was a Catholic and many Protestants fought him as if they were campaigning against the pope. Not so at the *Herald*. It remained neutral and measured its coverage of each candidate line by line. Its editorials avoided any semblance of political leaning.

The *Herald* threw its neutrality out the front door when it came to boxing. Jack Dempsey had lived in Provo for several years as a boy and called Salt Lake his hometown. Every day for weeks before the heavyweight championship fight with Gene Tunney, the paper ran a photo of Dempsey on its front page. When Tunney licked Dempsey, Provo went into mourning. More than 1,200 copies of a *Herald* Extra were hawked by crying newsboys after the fight.

The *Herald* was a fighting newspaper, but mostly on local issues such as schools, taxes and a new airport. A typical editorial battle took place in July of 1929. The *Herald* attacked Provo mayor Alma Van Wagenen for his stand against free public concerts by local bands. Summer and fall weekly band concerts had been a Provo tradition for nearly eighty years. Band members were paid less than thirty cents an hour by the city for their rehearsal and concert time. The mayor still adamantly opposed the concerts since the city was paying for them. The *Herald* then assailed the mayor for making two trips to California that would have more than paid for the concerts. It then conceded victory to the mayor with an ironic twist of logic— there would be no more free concerts as long as Van Wagenen was mayor. Voters took the tip. The mayor was soundly defeated in the following primary election.

Provo editors had total editorial freedom and neither Ed nor his brother Jim ever said a word about the news, editorial or other content of the paper. By 1929 the paper's masthead regularly carried the following statement:

> "Neither this newspaper nor any of its stockholders or officials has any connection whatever, directly or indirectly, with any political party, public utility, real estate promotion or other private business except the publication of newspapers devoted solely to disinterested public service."

Ed told his editors that this was the way that the Scripps League Newspapers would be run—unlike Scripps-Howard, which wrote editorials and dictated the national political policy of its papers from its headquarters.

By mid-1964 the *Herald* no longer stressed local coverage at the expense of important national and international news. It became a "complete" newspaper and positioned itself for greater expansion in content and circulation.

The newspaper represented not simply good journalism but Ed Scripps's most cherished policy: delegate authority to local editors and publishers and give them complete professional freedom. Also give them stock bonuses and praise for doing a good job. These policies became a cornerstone of the Scripps League.

The philosophical difference between Ed and E.W. was clear. In outlining the fundamental principle and spirit of his newspapers, grandfather E.W. wrote: "This principle, this spark of life and vitality and vigor, is a moral principle. As a whole body, my newspaper is as full of corruption, of weakness and immorality as is any human being. But despite the existence of these elements, there also exists the moral principle that I speak of. That moral principle is a spirit of protest . . ."

Ed rejected protest as his newspapers' guiding principle and spirit. He chose service to the community. This did not mean his papers eliminated protest. Their editorials rebuked people and events that threatened their communities. They took particular aim at public officials and others who did not serve the community well. But league papers sought the positive—to support better schools, help build needed roads, lead worthy public charity drives, and punish crime. To do this, Ed had to attract idealistic men and women. This was later to become his greatest strength— to choose able, fair leaders who would remain with the Scripps League.

E.W. wrote: "I grew by fighting, fighting because it is my nature to fight . . ."

A news colleague said of Ed: "Kindness is Ed Scripps's Achilles heel."

Ed is a reserved, thoughtful, bookish man and, although he liked boxing as a sport, he was always uncomfortable fighting others. He seeks peace through positive thinking and diligent effort.

Ed and his newspapers are now the antithesis of his grandfather's flamboyant approach to news and life. That is not necessarily the formula for success in newspapering. As a matter of fact, most newspapermen and women would say: The first duty of a newspaper is to raise hell.

Ed defies this view to a large extent. He believes that a newspaper should be a forum for opinion and not dictate its views to the community. Ed aims to free creativity, to inspire people, to develop their natural abilities. That means looking outward and changing society for the better.

Ed appreciates success stories—how someone achieved a goal. He believes in reporting at least as much "good works" as malicious crime. Ed concludes:

"I believe that newspapers are known by their works."

As they traveled together, Betty brought three new dimensions to Ed's personal and professional life—a loving atmosphere, a dynamic drive to learn the newspaper business, and natural leadership ability. Ed was profoundly in love with his wife when he married her. That love has deepened with the years.

Betty reflects on the early years: "I couldn't sit home while my husband was on the road. I loved our sons, Barry and Ed III, but my husband needed me. They were going to good schools and we had an excellent housekeeper. My parents lived nearby and supervised them. We also returned home regularly to keep close to them."

Ed and Betty Scripps traveled widely for the Scripps League, but still found time for their sons Ed, age 8, and Barry, age 5, circa 1955.

Ed and Betty took many family trips. These included ice skating at Sun Valley, Idaho, and Squaw Valley, California. The boys also accompanied them to Europe, the Hawaiian islands, Mexico and Canada. The family spent its summers at Lake Tahoe, where each boy had his own boat with an outboard motor. Actually, each of the sons built his own boat and bought motors as large as each could carry.

Betty had a Chris Craft speedboat and often raced it back and forth along Rubicon Beach as well as down to Emerald Bay and back. In later years, the sons used the Chris Craft.

Cal-Neva Lodge on the shoreline of Lake Tahoe was a favorite spot of the family. Frank Sinatra then owned the place. The nightclub featured a gaming casino as well as excellent floor shows and dinner. One evening Betty was playing roulette and Ed was at the slot machines. Sinatra entered and asked the club manager who the blonde broad was playing roulette. The manager quickly replied that Betty was the wife of Ed Scripps, the newspaper-chain owner, who was close by. He was hinting to Sinatra to lay off. Frank did. The manager, who knew the family well, later repeated the story to Betty, who laughed.

Betty recalls those years: "The newspaper world seemed to consume me. It was so much more than sitting by a pool or playing tennis or bridge. I couldn't stand to live without facing the challenge with Ed. I had to be part of it because it was so much of his life. My first thought and concern has always been Ed."

Ed recalls the early 1950s on the road with his wife: "Betty offered me love and stability, even more than I expected when we were married. I was mechanical, some say electronic, and theoretical. She was very practical. I was into computers early and thought of bringing a network onto our papers. She thought it better to wait until computers were more developed and their systems debugged. She made the right decision."

Ed recalls his wife's input: "Betty was a master of detail. She was very systematic and remembered everything. She carried a small notebook and made notes on things to do. She was also a good character analyst—who would work hard and who could be trusted. I was blessed with that gift, too. It was doubly hard to fool us. She was also very ambitious but so was I. Neither viewed the struggle to get ahead as a fault. As a matter of fact, ambition was necessary to keep us going. One of my favorite philosophical quotes was:

" 'Life is forever surpassing itself.' "

Betty began keeping a daily journal in 1954, not only to record what happened but to plan for tomorrow and the future. It now runs about 400 pages of notes, and is still growing.

Betty remembers: "Without ever discussing the subject, our marriage also became a business partnership. We were in love personally and with our professional lives. Too many newspaper families were fighting, going public, disappearing. We didn't want that. We wanted to keep our family and the business together.

"I became a self-educated newspaperwoman by years of study— writing, editing, composing, business, accounting, law, understanding the entire newspaper plant. I even wrote a column, which was later compiled into a book, on women's fashions. I never stopped reading about the business.

"We traveled a million miles by car and plane without an argument. Our secret was respect for each other's approach to life and a reluctance to impose one's views on the other."

When Ed and Betty returned home from trips, they spent extra time with their two sons by their first marriages—her Barry and his E.W. Scripps III. Ed adopted Barry when the youngster was nine years old.

In 1954 Betty expected their first child. The two curtailed traveling in anticipation of the joyous event. Ed was ecstatic and counted each day before the birth.

There were unexpected complications. Betty developed a dermoid cyst. In most cases, the cyst stops growing before the baby is born. After the birth, it begins to increase again and surgery removes it. In Betty's case, the cyst continued growing. Her physician planned to try to force the baby at seven months. Ed drove her to Palo Alto Hospital and didn't leave Betty's bedside for several days. The baby, a girl, was eventually born dead.

Betty and Ed were devastated. It was the most traumatic experience of their lives. They went home to Atherton, closed the doors, and suffered alone.

Ed's brother Jim finally suggested that Ed take Betty on a long sea voyage. The two packed and sailed for Brazil. Earlier in 1954, they had joined the Inter-American Press Association and now attended their first meeting. The trip opened a new door in their lives and began their lifelong interest in promoting the cause of a free press in Latin America.

By 1970 the couple's dream of twenty newspapers had been surpassed. Indeed, the goal was more than doubled. The Scripps League had over forty newspapers.

Some of these papers were in partnership with other owners, including longtime editors and publishers like Duane Hagadone, Phil Swift, Robert S. Howard and Platt Cline. All owned an original percentage of the paper or later gained one through stock options provided by Ed and Jim.

At the start of the 1960s, Ed was one of the first to go heavily into offset printing, which reduced the production cost for an average page by forty percent.

Les Wolfe, called by his colleagues on the Coeur d'Alene *Press* a "mechanical genius," set up a new process for moving stories and advertising more easily into offset (a process in which an inked impression from a plate is made on a rubber-blanketed cylinder and then transferred to newsprint) printing. Wolfe developed a composing room with people around a Lazy Susan pasting up news pages as a conveyor belt brought work to and from them. The system eliminated the need for editors and others to walk from one area to another. It was a big time and money saver. Editors sat at a single post and moved on and off line particular pages assigned them.

The electronics were also on line. Computers with stories and ads became a network or factory line. The system was adopted at Scripps League newspapers years before it was used at other papers.

The league's newspapers also were redesigned—not only their

The Coeur d'Alene *Press,* 1953.

layout but content. There were new sections on lifestyle, health and fitness, more business, sports, comics, and personal items. Editors remained in total control of the content of the news and editorial pages.

The rise of television news has changed the face of print journalism. Papers have instituted greater in-depth coverage, more investigative reporting, more extensive analysis of events, and added advocacy journalism, in which reporters substitute their own opinions for more objective news coverage. In one of the few times that Ed shaped local editorial policy, he banned any form of advocacy journalism.

Big-city afternoon papers had long been ravaged by the commuter flight from large cities, the new advertising power of radio and television, as well as the rise of suburban newspapers. On the other hand, community newspapers, many of which were afternooners, have thrived. This was especially true in the West, which lagged two and three hours behind Eastern time, allowing them to print late news from Washington and the New York stock market, as well as other late-breaking events in the East, including sports scores. It reduced the advantages of big-city morning papers trying to invade the league's territories in the West.

Meantime, Ed got mixed up with Dick Tracy and Mollie Slott. Tracy and Slott? Yes, the comic strip character and the brilliant executive editor of the New York Daily News-Chicago Tribune Syndicate. It was a heck of a fight. Gentle Ed came out swinging.

The Scripps League had signed a contract with the syndicate to receive Dick Tracy. However, Joe Patterson, who was running the *News* and the syndicate, bowed to pressures from larger clients. Big-city newspapers, including the Salt Lake City papers, wanted to shut out smaller papers within their circulation areas from obtaining comic strips and other syndicate features. Since they were higher-paying clients, Patterson cut off service to the Provo *Daily Herald* and any small paper that was challenged. Ed knew this would harm the *Herald*'s circulation.

So Ed sued Patterson and the syndicate on antitrust grounds. Patterson wouldn't budge. He would wait out this small-town rube

The pressroom of
the Coeur d'Alene
Press, 1955.

and eventually stuff him in a pile of hay. But the yokel hired high-powered attorneys and went to court. Patterson waited. The hayseed would run out of money. But Ed didn't and the case continued for weeks. It was clear that Patterson was going to lose the case. So the New Yorker called off his lawyers and settled out of court. The country bumpkin had conquered the towering *News* on Forty-second Street, and Provo got Dick Tracy.

Meantime, brother Jim, the math wizard, continued to work his ingenuity on behalf of the League and its papers. Each newspaper was becoming more financially solid. Jim was so good at abstract thinking that he took up telephone chess. It was no small feat to keep the entire changing board in his mind.

In the early 1970s, notes of disharmony began to arise between the brothers. Jim would want to buy a new paper. Ed wouldn't. Ed would suggest a personnel change. Jim expressed doubt and wouldn't agree. A series of disagreements developed. Nothing serious. No shouting. No anger expressed. But for the first time in their lives—some six decades—tension began to grow between the two men. No one could pinpoint the reasons for the uneasiness but it intensified. A blowup was coming, an explosion that some would view as almost as great as the split between their father Jim and his brother Robert. As grandfather E.W. put it long before, it was in the nature of the Scrippses to fight.

The composing room of the Coeur d'Alene *Press,* 1955.

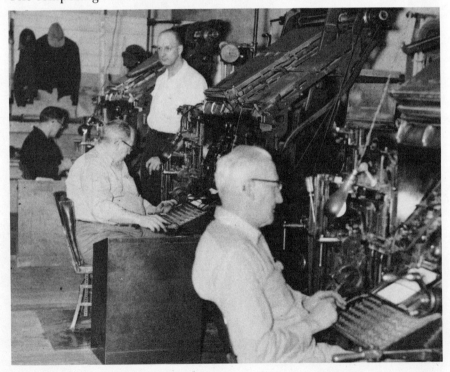

THE SPINOFF

In 1969, after nearly four decades of expanding the organization, Jim suggested that the Scripps League go public. The idea of selling stock in the firm outside the family hit Ed like an Arctic blast. He had always viewed the league as a private company that was part of a century-old commitment of the Scrippses to newspapering. Ed also saw the league as a long-term investment that would be passed on to future generations of the family.

Ed knew that the times may have been against him. Many private companies, including some of the nation's largest and most traditional firms, were now issuing stock. For one reason or another, they needed cash—to expand, limit debt or bring new blood into their leadership.

Going public made Ed very uneasy. He discussed it with Betty. They tentatively decided against the proposition for two reasons— the league didn't need the money and the family could ultimately lose financial and administrative control of the league. Ed held

Betty Knight Scripps
at the Scrippses' Hills-
borough home, 1968.

controlling interest in the company's stock while Jim and sister
Ellen were minority shareholders. Ed had been company president
and board chairman since the league was incorporated by his
mother in 1931. His sister Josephine had long since sold her
interest in the company in order to buy Fanita Ranch, where she
ran a dairy farm and raised bulls. (Josephine eventually decided
that Fanita was impossible to manage because it was so big and was
invaded by neighbors' cattle and had other problems. She sold the
property in 1967 and bought the smaller Hi-Hope Ranch near
Oceanside.)

Ed didn't recognize that a major new family conflict was about
to explode. Jim was headed for a company showdown. Such a
possibility was always conceivable; however, Ed felt that Jim, not
only his brother but his closest friend apart from Betty, would

never contemplate such an action. The two brothers had faced one business challenge after another over the years and were bound by a bond of mutual trust and respect. There had rarely been a harsh word between them. The same went for Ellen. She had devoted decades to the company as a top bookkeeper. Ellen knew that the league and the name Scripps were a tradition in American journalism. Such a confrontation was crazy, Ed told himself. It was nuts!

Ed waited. He saw no reason to take a position on any speculative thoughts by his brother. Months passed. Jim had apparently dropped the subject after Ed told him that he didn't see any immediate or particular reason to go public.

About a year later, in 1970, Ellen indicated that she was joining Jim's proposal to sell stock outside the company. Her announcement dropped on Ed like a bomb. Why? he asked. What was the advantage? What about the league's future? The name Scripps?

As a result of Ed's questions—and indirect objections—Jim wrote several memos to his brother in which Jim was clearly of two minds about going public. Ellen was a different story. Ed discovered that Ellen was maneuvering behind the scenes, needling Jim to break with their brother. Ellen had always been closer to Jim than to Ed, but Ed was still surprised. They were not enemies. As far as he knew, Ellen didn't want to control the league. Nor did she appear to need money.

Jim and Ellen probed Ed to see if he would relinquish control of the company. They and unnamed partners would buy him out. Ed was startled. In their long relationship, he never had the slightest inkling that the two wanted to take command of the newspapers. Associates asked why Ellen and Jim did not combine their stock and force Ed from power. The two held the majority only in non-voting stock (Class A). Ed always owned fifty-one percent of the voting shares (Class B) while Jim held forty-nine percent of the voting shares.

Jim and Ellen asked Ed for his views regarding the future of the company. Ed had waited patiently for that precise question. He said that he soon planned to give Betty fifty percent of his stock. Jim and Ellen sputtered disbelief. Neither was close to Betty. Their incredulity turned to rage. Ed could not do that. Yes, Ed said mildly, that was precisely what he would do shortly.

Ellen and Betty, in particular, had never gotten along. Ed recalls: "Betty was intelligent and pretty. Ellen was intelligent but older and not a beautiful woman. Nor did she have Betty's social grace. Ellen was very jealous of Betty and would not even speak to her."

Ed was still shaking his head when Ellen hit him with a financial broadside. She wanted to cash in her company stocks and leave the league. Ellen's stock was worth $11 million, according to a previous "memo-balance" financial agreement whereby the trio valued their respective assets in the league. She asked that Ed buy her out and demanded nearly $30 million, almost three times the estimated value of her stock.

The situation became extremely sensitive. Ed says that Ellen threatened to go to court and dissolve the league. She might claim mismanagement and offer a dozen other complaints. The company could be tied up in litigation for years. Ellen would show Betty who the real queen of the Scripps League was.

Ed was convinced that Ellen would carry out her threat. He says Ellen had a series of personal quirks and problems during her life which caused her to be unpredictable. Ed recalled that their mother had objected to some of the men in his sister's life, including her husband.

Ed then hired Lloyd Cutler, one of Washington's "super" lawyers. He was a partner in the prestigious firm of Wilmer, Cutler & Pickering. Cutler warned Ed and Betty that the confrontation with Ellen could turn into a family scandal if Ellen went to court. "She'll pull you down," Cutler said. "You're not going to pull her up."

Jim took no part in Ellen's threats or behavior toward Betty. That is why Ed was stunned when he received Jim's harsh letter of June 8, 1974, criticizing his wife. It was the most intemperate—perhaps also the pettiest—rebuke of Betty by a member of the Scripps family in her twenty-four years as a member of it:

"... Although I disagree with Ellen, my regard and respect for her is minimally influenced by her current intransigent thinking that, in the event of your death or disability, she cannot get along with Betty. I have tried, perhaps in error, to mediate. Ellen's view, voiced to me by phone today is: 'I cannot face the prospect of dealing with Betty. I believe Ed is honorable and will treat me honorably. I propose to communicate with him directly and ask him what kind of deal he can make to deal with my interests.'

". . . Basically, Ellen and I are flabbergasted and confounded by your decision as to disposition of those twenty-six shares (the controlling stock of the Scripps League). Yesterday, I mentioned the fact that, to me, the timing didn't make sense. You have a son going on thirty-three. You have a stepson (adopted is accurate) going on thirty. Now, with a wife without business qualifications or background, you had faith that she should decide within a few years where the stock should go; this would add up if teenage sons were involved. There seems to be a general picture of a housewife starting out at age forty-eight to learn the business and either decide between sons in a few years—or decide between her grandchildren and your grandchildren at the age of around seventy-four. Neither seems to add up.

"Now, getting on as to particulars, I will ask you to go way, way back and remember that you asked me, before you married Mary Oldham, what my opinion was. I distinctly recall advising against the marriage solely on the ground, as communicated to me, that Mary did not like children. Maybe you remember this. Maybe you don't. I won't say you were wrong in that marriage. If there is any disagreement there, it is that you have perhaps minimized the value of the genes of your descendants as applicable to all children, considering the standing of Mary's father and Mary's obviously good I.Q. The most unacceptable thing in relations between any two human beings is to be right. Perhaps you will not recall or agree with my recollections as above, but it is my distinct recollection that Mary broke off one of her children's front teeth by swatting her in the face with a hair brush. No more on Mary or your first marriage.

"Now, as to Betty—and I may be a damn fool to write this letter. You didn't ask me about this marriage. If she has given you happiness, you deserve it. As to her parents, to cover the whole field . . . I have a deep respect and admiration for Eleanor (Betty's mother). I disagree with the theory that she speaks great French. (Perhaps I am wrong.) I am sure she has been a good mother to Betty. I admire and respect Betty's good treatment of her mother. On the other hand, to have everything

Betty with her mother's friends at a fundraising party in Hillsborough, 1968.

in the open, I must admit to some dislike of Howard Knight (Betty's father). I recall once writing a letter saying that people in the concern considered him as phony as a three-dollar bill . . . I have a very strong personal grievance. I love my wife. I stand ready to take a lie detector test that she has never in her life been insulted as gratuitously and grossly as by Howard Knight. This is an admission of grounds for prejudice, so it should be noted.

"However, first going back to that matter of age—as having some bearing on her suitability as your heir—I must admit I never stopped to think when I assumed she was about four years older than she is. Just a couple of months ago, you showed me her passport when we met in New York—and the facts happened to fall into place. Betty's birthday and Barry's birthday established that Barry was conceived when she was eighteen years old. This obviously was in complete contradiction to her publicity releases about attending Stanford, being involved with Stanford sororities (of which there were none), being a member of the Junior League, etc. Talking about an age a few years down the line was apparently part of the scenario—and I should have noticed it at the time.

". . . The next item which causes me extreme concern is your expression to me some years back of extreme exasperation with the People's Bank when they sent a statement to your home instead of to your office so that Betty figured you had some extra money—and promptly spent it. The plain inference was that you considered Betty to be financially profligate. A very bad recommendation for a person to succeed to ultimate responsibility in control of a firm headed for the $100 million rank.

"Another item, again from your own words in a meeting with Ellen and me, relates to the event of Barry personally handing a substantial foundation gift to the president of the University of Arizona at Tucson just prior to his getting graduated. To me, this was an obvious impropriety. I distinctly recall your saying that this was Betty's idea.

"As very minor items, there are recent mentions by Betty of her position on the board of the San Francisco Symphony as relating to her managerial qualifications. It was hard for me not to choke on this, considering the foundation donations to the symphony.

"Going back further, relating to Betty's (Scripps newspapers) column, Marion and I happened to run across a column by a prestigious though rather oddball writer who had an item about a chick standing on a street corner. It happened to be copyrighted. This is an article of record and Betty cribbed it and, under practice at that time, it was sent in for a second copyright. I didn't bother you about it at the time—but is this the kind of thing that earns precedence for seniority in a business structure?

"Again, my most recent shock was a careful survey by (our) family of Betty's recent articles for the concern. Very few printed. I mentioned papers and dates. One an obvious handout. The other an obvious clipping that she had not bothered to read—nor did the person sending it out—nor did the paper printing it.

". . . It is obvious to me that the picture to be drawn is that Betty doesn't only not write a good many of her articles, but she doesn't even READ them. And still we are paying $18,000 per year and you have her named as heir apparent.

"I hope the above supplies some data. I admit to prejudice. But now is the time to speak out—as we must work out some treaty to have a unified concern—or else figure out how best to outline an equitable division."

Ed was in shock when he finished reading the letter. He concluded that Ellen had so filled Jim with her envy of Betty that the situation had turned to blind hatred. He was also convinced that Ellen had turned Jim's wife Marion against Betty. Ed confesses that he had never witnessed such personal animosity.

Ed was too much of a gentleman to show the cruelly worded personal attack to Betty. Yet his wife had faced such family opposition and acrimony from the start of their marriage. Even Betty's sharpest critics admitted, however, that she never replied to those who picked her apart—not a word. She conducted her life with great grace.

Ed never responded to Jim's letter, but he privately answered the accusations. Steadily but quietly, for some twenty-four years, Betty had been studying and, in many instances, actively taking part in most aspects of his news operations. This included writing fashion stories so that she would get a clearer perspective on reporting. Betty was not, as the letter claimed, a housewife starting out at age forty-eight trying to learn about newspaper publishing. She had become experienced over nearly a quarter-century of continuous work.

If she had differences with Ellen, no one ever heard any of them from Betty.

The timing of Barry's birth established nothing about Betty's attendance at Stanford, sororities, or her being a member of the Junior League. Betty was graduated from Burlingame High School in the summer of 1943 after three-and-one-half years of study. She then attended Drews Summer School in San Francisco and took the aptitude test for Stanford the same year. She was accepted at the university. She went to San Mateo College in the fall in order to enter Stanford as a sophomore. Betty attended many Stanford functions and advised the university that she planned to formalize its acceptance in her second college year. All of this occurred before Betty was eighteen. She dropped out of school to marry the following year. Barry was born to her three weeks after her nineteenth birthday.

Regarding Jim's reference to the Junior League, Betty was a

member of the Children's Theater Association, which was founded by the Junior League. He may have been confused on this point.

Without documenting his case, for Jim to suggest that Betty was embellishing her background—and for a very brief period in her life at that—was at best a cheap shot.

Jim claimed that Betty opened Ed's bank statements on several occasions. He also accused Betty of "profligate" spending. Jim said both claims were based on casual conversations with Ed. Ed flatly denies that either conversation ever took place. He says the accusations were part of a pattern of criticism of his wife. For Jim to claim that Ed would criticize Betty to him is contrary to every aspect of Ed's well-established character. Ed felt that his brother had intruded into the relationship between a husband and wife, which was sacred to him. Neither Ed nor Betty ever inserted themselves into Jim's relationship with his wife. Nor did they ever comment to others on Jim's very heavy drinking—corroborated by members of Jim's own staff—or various incidents involving Jim's wife, Marion.

The two were linked to a letter written by John Paul Scripps's wife, Edith, in 1969 to Barry Scripps's bride-to-be. The letter said that "Barry was not a Scripps" although he had been legally adopted by Ed as his son in 1953. This hurt Barry deeply. Ed and Betty were also offended by this but they said nothing.

As a result of that letter, Betty's father, Howard Knight, threatened to sue Edie, as she was known, for defamation of character. That upset Jim and Marion as well as other members of the family who did not like Betty, Barry's mother.

Jim and Marion were said to dislike Howard Knight for a second reason. Betty was told by the publisher of the league paper in Honolulu that Marion indicated Betty had toured the country as a singer with the Ted Weems band in 1941. Betty says the story was untrue and she was mortified by it. She was only sixteen at the time and her parents never would have permitted her to be on the road alone. Knight became angry and went to friends in San Francisco, accusing Marion of false gossip. The charge soon filtered back to Jim and Marion, who dropped the story.

Ed thought that his brother's comments about the conduct of

Betty and Ed and her parents, Mr. and Mrs. C. Howard Knight, at the opening of the San Francisco Opera, 1968.

Betty's father—good or bad—was another unwarranted family intrusion. Knight's comportment had nothing to do with the company or its decisions. He says Jim and his wife were clearly out of bounds in both these incidents.

Jim's reference to the league foundation gift to the University of Arizona at Barry's graduation was hardly an "impropriety." Barry was leaving the university. He sought nothing of it then or since.

The league foundation did contribute funds to the San Francisco Symphony, and Betty became a symphony board member. That is hardly new or unusual. People who contribute to such institutions are often sought for such boards precisely because of their interest.

Betty's extensive travel and long hours on fashion stories argue against Jim's claim that she cribbed articles from other writers. Avon Books, which checked the material, published them in book form.

The bottom line was that Jim's letter offered no proof of his allegations, and therefore lacked the substantiation that is basic to a professional journalist's work.

On reflection, Ed concluded that Jim's letter left him no choice—it would be necessary for him, his brother and sister to work out an equitable division of the company. The decision deeply saddened him.

Ed remonstrated with himself that perhaps he should have seen the split coming. He somehow might have been able to head it off. For several years, the brothers had had an increasing number of policy disagreements—not only about taking the company public but the purchase of newspapers and operational issues. In trying to buy more papers, Jim sought more control and power although he continued to own a minority interest in the company. For example, Jim wanted to purchase papers in Elizabeth, New Jersey, Haverhill, Massachusetts, and Beckley, West Virginia. Ed did not. He was not impressed by these papers and wanted to avoid the debt.

Ed felt that Jim was on a solo ego trip—that the partnership had worked well because the two complemented one another, not moved in different directions. Jim was exceptionally gifted in financial matters and worked hard at creating the loyalty of business associates. Ed was convinced he was a much better judge of executive talent, superior in editorial judgment, and a much more astute final decision-maker. He was unquestionably a far greater mechanical or technological mind in operating the papers.

While the brothers discussed their differences, Jim quietly informed the league's top managers—Duane Hagadone, Robert S. Howard, Phil Buckner, and Phil Swift—that they might do better by joining him in either taking over the league or dividing it between himself and Ed. The publishers owned nonvoting stock and, even if some decided to do so, they could not help Jim take over the company. Yet all were powerful forces within the league.

The Hagadone family had been with the company for more than forty years. Buckner was with the firm thirty and Swift more than twenty. Howard had been with the company for six years. Jim also suggested he would give them greater power and profit in any new organization. This set off behind-the-scenes scurrying among the quartet about their future.

The four split about joining Jim. One reason was the league had paid them exceptionally good stock bonuses. It was doubtful that Jim could offer more. Some had become millionaires while working for the league. The four viewed the differences between Ed and Jim this way:

They believed that Ed and Jim's "estate planning" was a major reason for the brothers' growing alienation. Since Ed and Jim were in their sixties, it made good sense for each to provide for his heirs while not under the pressure of any crisis or death. Most saw Ed's offering Betty fifty percent of his stock as the major conflict. Jim and Ellen wanted no working relationship with Betty. Jim always denied that his estate planning had anything to do with the breakup.

The four also concluded that each brother wished to exercise the crucial decision-making power in the firm. All were also aware that the brothers disagreed over whether to buy certain papers. The four themselves didn't agree on whether to purchase particular new papers. All had a history of competing for Ed and Jim's attention. Finally, all had long known that the brothers' wives didn't get along, but none had measured the full extent of Ellen's hatred of Betty. Nor did they know of Ellen's financial demands.

Distance was another factor in the breakdown of the brothers' rapport. Jim had moved with his wife and two daughters to the San Juan Islands off Puget Sound while Ed remained in California. The two didn't see one another as often as when they lived in Seattle and California. Business was conducted by phone and letter. This combination made their relationship much more remote.

The four Scripps executives decided to spin off from the league and go their own ways. It was not a quick decision for any of them. Duane Hagadone's father, Burl, had worked for Ed over a long stretch in earlier years. Duane himself began working for the league when he was ten years old. He learned the business by doing odd jobs at the Coeur d'Alene *Press* through high school. Duane left college to become director of advertising and circulation at the *Press*. When Burl Hagadone died, Duane became publisher of the *Press* at the age of twenty-six. He later oversaw other Scripps papers.

Hagadone says he left the league to launch his own company because he felt the firm's business outlook had become too conservative. Ed was not saddened by the decision. He says Hagadone wanted to pile up too much company debt, while Ed was burdened with most of the risk. Duane wanted to borrow $16 million to expand eleven league papers under him. Hagadone told the Scrippses that he had secured the loan at the Jefferson Pilot Insurance Company in Durham, North Carolina. Ed, Betty and Barry went to Durham to meet with Jack Warmath, president of Jefferson Pilot and a company lawyer. In the meeting, Betty suddenly asked if the proposed agreement was a double-collateral loan. Hagadone already had a loan against the papers and the new accord would represent an additional responsibility. Such an agreement would have put the other six league papers at risk as well as the family's personal estate and savings. Warmath affirmed that it was a double-collateral pact. Stunned, Betty stood and said:

"The deal is off."

She turned to Ed, who had already risen, and Barry, who had just begun to get out of his chair. The three thanked Warmath for his candor and walked out of the office. However, all felt less than appreciative toward Hagadone. Later, a Jefferson attorney was quoted as saying:

"Betty would never give away the family jewels."

Ed and Betty were also told that Ed's sister Ellen had planned to ask for the six papers in exchange for her league stock. Betty believed that Hagadone contemplated teaming up with Ellen to run the papers and eventually buy her out.

Betty stood up and rebelled at the Jefferson meeting because she believed Hagadone had double-crossed them—in more ways than one. It marked the first time, since Ed began teaching her the news business twenty-seven years earlier, that she publicly led the way in a

Ed and his sons, from left: Barry, Ed, and Ed III at the La Jolla Beach Club.

major company decision. It was a signal to everyone outside the family that the new half-owner of the league was someone to be reckoned with.

Hagadone was the last of the four to split with the league, leaving in 1977. He now owns the *Press* and six other daily papers in Idaho, another paper in partnership with Bob Howard, as well as many other businesses in Coeur d'Alene, a resort community in the foot-hills of the Bitterroot Mountains.

Bob Howard viewed the league's split from an entirely different perspective. Howard felt the two brothers and their mother had been dealt a dirty deal by E.W. He said: "They should have inherited more, perhaps the entire Scripps-Howard empire. Instead, Charles Scripps became the big inheritor."

Bob Howard wanted to launch his own newspaper chain and left the league on good terms. He now owns nineteen dailies in California and other Western states.

In 1975 Phil Swift left as publisher of the Napa *Register*. He took the league's Lake Tahoe and Roseburg (Oregon) newspapers in return for his stock. He now runs his own small newspaper chain. Swift also ran papers for Jim Scripps in the early 1980s.

Buckner, who was financially well-off when he joined the league, formed the Buckner Newspaper Alliance and maintained a partnership with Jim Scripps until 1986. The two were close friends. Buckner also owned the Lewiston (Pennsylvania) *Sentinel* with the Scripps League until 1987.

Some of the quartet's associates offer another reason for the league's split—that neither Ed nor Jim was convinced he had produced a strong heir. Jim had two daughters, neither of whom had any aspiration at the time to head a newspaper chain. Ed's son, E.W. Scripps III, had not distinguished himself as a student or newspaperman. Some compared Betty's son, Barry, to Hagadone. The two were measured against one another because it appeared that Barry was being groomed for a top executive post in the league. One reason for that was, he showed much more courage than his brother Ed III when his father and mother faced the traumatic days of the spinoff. The four associates saw Barry as lacking much of Duane's experience, skills and aggressive drive.

The comparison between Barry and Hagadone lingered over the league for a long time. One company executive put it this way: " 'Hag' was lean and mean. If he bought the New York Yankees, he would try to play with only seven men to save on salaries. Despite that, he was likable. He was a go-go guy. He was smart, worked hard, and you respected him. Barry came across as a personable playboy."

The comparison with Hagadone was unfair because of the Idahoan's many years in the business. His all-out, go-get-'em business attitude was a unique personal and professional quality.

The crisis came to a head when all four top executives told the Scripps brothers that each thought he could do better on his own. Ed thus faced: Jim's movement to divide the league; Ellen's threat to dissolve the organization unless she received a cash settlement worth nearly three times that of her company stock; and the fact that these longtime partners and newspaper executives planned to pull out of the league. With the company appearing to be splintering in three different directions, no one, including Ed, could foresee the consequences. The future looked bleak.

After several phone arguments, Ed and Jim began communicating through their lawyers. Jim was thus no longer an intermediary between Ed and Ellen. The sister started speaking through her attorneys as well. It was an ugly family flareup, reminiscent of the arguments between E.W., his brothers and, later, his wife and sons. A slew of nasty rumors blossomed on the the league grapevine. Questions persisted: Who was in charge of the papers? Who would be? What would be the fate of each paper? What would happen to the employees?

Meantime, in 1969, Barry had been graduated from the University of Arizona's Journalism School. He went to work in the advertising department of the Napa *Register* for the next year and a half. He subsequently worked in other departments of the paper. In 1971 Barry was named publisher of the league's Banning-Beaumont (California) *Record-Gazette*, a 3,000-circulation daily. He served there two years before becoming a league vice president.

In 1975, with the league collapsing, Barry was named its executive vice president. Because of the mounting problems, Ed was unable to spend much time traveling to meet with the individual newspaper staffs. He needed at least one son to help him.

Barry soon tried to patch up the partnership with Hagadone, who, partly because he inherited much from his father, was a relatively large league stockholder. As Barry explained it: "Duane was on a power trip. He cared about his image. He wanted his name on everything. My father allowed Hagadone Newspapers on the masthead of the league papers which Duane operated. My father said it was fine with him if Duane wanted to use his own name on the papers, but he must be successful. Ed didn't care about personal publicity. But he did want Duane to remember that he worked for him."

Barry failed to keep Hagadone in the league because Duane wanted his own newspaper chain and was interested in other businesses. The reason was not so much that Barry couldn't convince Hagadone to stay. Rather, it was Duane's own widespread ambitions, much beyond that of the media, and the fact that Ed had killed Hagadone's attempt to have the company accept more heavy debt. Duane had long been ready to go off on his own. Hagadone was a very aggressive individual and his decision to leave was a good personal choice, since his go-get-'em business approach has been highly successful. It's jokingly said that Hagadone now owns half of Coeur d'Alene. That's not far from wrong. In addition to owning seven of the eight newspapers in northern Idaho, Hagadone is owner of another paper with Bob Howard, and runs Coeur d'Alene's two radio stations. He commands a large amount of choice land in the area as well as the only resort on Lake Coeur d'Alene. Hagadone also owns two lake marinas, a golf course with a floating green, and the local Yellow Pages. Local businessmen call Coeur d'Alene a company town—Hagadone's. T-shirts are sold locally with a caricature of Duane on the front shouting against the backdrop of the city: "Mine! Mine! Mine!"

Hagadone indeed has tried to maneuver and control much of what has occurred among Coeur d'Alene's 25,000 residents. *The Wall Street Journal* reported in 1992 that he got the county commission to cut his taxes while those of nearly everyone else climbed. Hagadone has taken members of the Boise legislature to lunch en masse when he wanted something done, including approval of racetrack gambling in the state. Perhaps his greatest lobbying achievement was cajoling the Coeur d'Alene town council into allowing him to construct an eighteen-story tower for his resort—despite a three-story height restriction and outspoken public opposition.

The background on Hagadone is significant because some past executives of the Scripps League maintain that Ed entrusted too much power to some of his early managers, such as Duane. Barry Scripps insists that power is the focal point of Hagadone's business practices.

Before Jim finally left the league, Duane and Phil Swift's spinoffs

occurred. Previous to that, however, they favored buying the Elizabeth and Haverhill papers. Ed abhorred buying Elizabeth's because
the 66,000-circulation daily was a "dog." Under pressure from Jim
and his associates, however, he agreed to do so.

The Elizabeth newspaper was heavily unionized and Ed antici-
pated trouble. The city of Elizabeth also was going nowhere. The
paper was later hit with a strike in 1978 and lost 25,000 readers. It
was eventually sold at a big loss and, after a string of owners, closed
in 1991. The deal cost Ed a bundle. However, due to the purchase,
Jim, Hagadone and Swift received a higher percentage of stock
when they left the company.

Just why Ed agreed to buy the papers, particularly Elizabeth's,
has never been clear. He never relied on anyone else's judgment but
his own in purchasing a paper. Ed was always very independent in
his business decisions. In retrospect, it appears Ed may have gone
along to see if he could keep Hagadone and Swift as league execu-

Ed and Betty Scripps and author Arthur Hailey and his wife Sheila at the
opening of the San Francisco Opera.

tives. Ed shakes his head about the decision today. He appears to blame no one but himself for it.

Barry, on the other hand, saw the Elizabeth and Haverhill pressures on Ed as a power play. He claims that Jim, Hagadone and Swift thought Ed would be so disgusted by the deal that he would sell his stock and Jim would take over the company with the two others as his top assistants. Such a thought may have crossed Swift's mind because Jim had discussed making him his top aide in any new company. It seems improbable, however, that Hagadone would have followed Barry's scenario because of his own plans and ambitions.

Jim and Ellen seemed to have a more subtle plan to oust Ed. With Jim attempting to get the top four executives to join him or sell out and Ellen demanding almost $30 million cash for her stock, the two were unquestionably squeezing Ed financially. This was the kind of well-planned ploy that E.W. used on family members and associates when he wanted to remove them from his business.

Barry hung tough. He told his parents: "I will do whatever we have to do to save the company."

Barry says he eventually fired Swift as the Napa publisher although Phil planned to leave. Barry traveled around the country attempting to shore up the loyalty and morale of various newspaper executives and staffs. That was not easy because he was forced to freeze executive and staff pay for three years and cut the payroll at virtually all papers. He also was not allowed to spend much on capital expenditures. It was a thankless job but hundreds of jobs, multimillion dollars, and the future of the league were at stake.

Barry's marriage also was on the line. During the league crisis, Barry's wife Katherine began complaining that he was making too many sacrifices for his business and parents. She was upset because he was on the road for long periods. She also didn't like the newspaper ambiance and thought Barry was too close to his family. Unknown to his colleagues, while trying to shore up the league, Barry was attempting to save his marriage.

After the company had regained its strength, Barry stepped down as executive vice president in the spring of 1984. It was too late. His wife took their three children and walked out in January of 1985. She later obtained a divorce and remarried. Barry has rewed happily and has two children by his second wife, Gail. He has become much more astute about the news business and been an even harder worker ever since. He was recently invited to join the International Young Presidents Organization.

In contrast to Barry's fight for the company, Ed Scripps III was a big question mark. He had gone to college in Switzerland but didn't finish. His performance at newspapers where he worked, including the tourist publications in Honolulu, was reported to be lackluster. Colleagues also said that he drank heavily.

At the height of the crisis, Ed III reportedly visited his Uncle Jim. For what reason? His parents say Ed III has never adequately explained the meeting. The son argued constantly and never seemed to agree with his father on business matters.

Ed III's wife Bonnie apparently did not get along with Ed and Betty. In turn, they viewed her as insensitive to the family's problems during the crisis and felt she would create trouble for everyone down the road. Bonnie subsequently took their two children and left Ed III. The couple have separated. Ed III, who has had two heart attacks, lives in Los Altos, California.

Betty recalls Ed III's role during the company shakeout: "When the chips were down, Ed III simply wasn't as strong as Barry. He wasn't supportive. He was a doubter. He couldn't be counted on to help. When some of the publishers left, Ed III said that everyone was deserting us. There were times when Ed III actually gave up. He told us:

" 'Let's sell out. That's the only thing that we can do.' "

Ed III now runs the small league newspapers in Taft, California, and Hamilton, Montana. He once described himself to colleagues at a league meeting in California:

"I am the black sheep of the family."

With the four publishers announcing that they were going their own ways, Jim finally concluded that his options were limited. Ed held the upper hand by controlling the voting stock. Eventually, Jim would have only one recourse—to exchange his company stock with Ed for some of the league newspapers. Jim vowed that would not happen without hard bargaining. However, Jim had lost the legal document that allowed him to spin off papers in the event that he and Ed agreed to split. Amid the temper of those times, with the two brothers talking only through their lawyers, Ed could have been as difficult to deal with as his brother and sister. If vindictiveness were part of the game, Ed could have asked Jim to produce the accord. He did not and the two brothers agreed in principle in August of 1975 to go their own ways. The agreement was finalized by their lawyers in April of 1977, but the settlement of all details was not completed until September 19, 1978.

It was necessary to clear the deal with the Internal Revenue Service. In a letter to the IRS on April 5, 1977, Jim's attorney reported that "serious management differences" had arisen between the brothers who were major shareholders in the firm. The statement added significant inside detail to the split:

"E.W. Scripps has informed his brother that he intends to leave his controlling interest to his wife and sons. James G. Scripps has taken the position that he does not feel that these three individuals have the ability to assume management control in the future, and that the management control should be placed in trust and that, while Betty Knight Scripps and the two sons would participate in the decision making process, they would be guided by James G. Scripps and the experienced executives of SLNI (Scripps League Newspapers, Inc.) and its professional advisors who have over the years contributed so heavily to the success and growth of SLNI. E.W. Scripps feels that this is management 'by committee' and would produce adverse results and is adamantly opposed to this policy. James G. Scripps has also taken the position that with the advancement of Betty Knight Scripps and Barry H. Scripps into executive positions they have, in the exercise of their authority, been placed in a position that conflicts with areas of authority which James G. Scripps thinks should be reserved to himself and other associates.

"The relationships among the substantial shareholders and among James G. Scripps and the members of his family have so far deteriorated that they are unable to proceed in a businesslike manner with respect to the normal operations of the business. Each of the two brothers maintains a position which is inconsistent with and incompatible with the other.

"The above arguments have ... become impossible and various members of the management team have in fact chosen sides in the above disputes. The disputes have had and will continue to have a progressively adverse effect upon SLNI's business and upon the morale of its management ...

"To summarize, the two voting shareholders of this corporation are deeply enmeshed in a bitter controversy concerning the present and future management of the corporation and its related properties. The only viable solution is to separate the contestants ... whose positions have become irreconcilable."

The complex 1978 agreement provided not only how the newspapers would be divided, but an intricate maze of financial structuring and responsibility. The deal almost collapsed at the last minute because Jim wanted Ed to accept the league's Coos Bay (Oregon) *World* in the division of league papers. The Newspaper Guild was threatening a strike at Coos Bay. Jim was convinced that management would not only lose the battle but a lot of money in the process. The union wanted higher pay, increased benefits, and more independence from management. They vowed to close the *World* down for a long time if their demands were not met. After years of bickering over details of their agreement, Jim told Ed through his lawyers:

"If you will accept Coos Bay, we have a deal."

Ed accepted the *World* and told the guild: "Go walk. We'll get the paper out."

Ed recalls: "I was never scared of the guild. I took them on in Seattle, Napa and elsewhere. The main reason was, the more benefits that the union won, the more its members became biased in reporting and writing and independent in other ways. The Coos Bay guild knew that I would never back down from a fight."

Jim was wrong. The union soon capitulated and a strike was averted. The guild knew that Ed would replace every one of their members. His attitude never changed:

"I never wanted anyone else controlling my newspapers."

Ed has been tough toward the guild throughout his career. The basic reason is that he believes the union virtually killed the Cleveland *Press*, the finest newspaper that his grandfather ever owned. Ed is extremely critical of his Uncle Bob and Roy Howard for "capitulating" to the union during the strike that broke the *Press*'s back.

Jim took over complete ownership of nine league papers in his spinoff. He formed a new chain called Pioneer Newspapers, which included the *Herald Journal* in Logan, Utah, the Idaho *State Journal* in Pocatello, Idaho, and the *Daily Chronicle* in Bozeman, Montana. After the division was finalized, Jim told friends: "I never really wanted the split. It served no real purpose."

As an indication of how Ed fared as a result of the spinoff, the league had thirty-six papers in 1981, including twenty-two dailies. He not only remained on his feet after the crisis, but strengthened the organization since the final settlement three years earlier.

Some business associates claim that Jim's wife, Marion, was as responsible as anyone for the spinoff. They say that her dislike of Betty Scripps was so great that she poisoned her husband's mind toward Ed and his family. They report that Marion's feelings were reflected in the stinging, sarcastic letter about Betty which Jim wrote to Ed on June 4, 1974.

Despite being repeated many times, that version of events does not square with the facts. Jim clearly made proposals to some of the league's top publishers to join him in a coup d'état against Ed. He sought to control the league. Some former associates now either refuse to admit that or will confirm it only indirectly and privately. During the three-year negotiations before the split occurred, Jim had more than sufficient time to reflect on what he was doing. Jim also was more than sixty years old at the time of the spinoff, with wide newspaper and business experience. To suggest that Marion shared equal responsibility with her husband for the breakup is an untenable leap of logic.

Although Josephine had died nearly twenty years before, she would have grieved at her sons' split. They had worked together for fifty-seven years.

Jim died on December 27, 1986, at Del Mar, California. His wife had passed away earlier. The couple's two daughters, Susan Scripps Wood and Sally Scripps, were left the Pioneer Newspapers. In true Scripps fashion, Susan Scripps Wood bought out her sister in 1991. Pioneer has three dailies, two tri-weeklies, and three weeklies, in contrast to the league's current eighteen dailies, twenty-five weeklies and other publications.

Ed and Betty's battle with Ellen was much more intense and emotional. In fact, both admit they awoke nights because of the strain of developments and found themselves writing one another notes about solving the dispute.

In new private meetings with Ed—Ellen still refused to see Betty—the sister continued to blister her brother's wife. Ellen apparently still viewed her sister-in-law as a Betty-come-lately who had not earned or deserved a place in the Scripps family. Ellen was a thin woman with a pinched, plain face and watery, weak eyes. Compared to Betty, Ellen's appearance was nondescript. Much of her unpleasantness stemmed from the fact that her brother had married a bright, energetic, good-looking woman sixteen and one-half years younger than himself. Ed and Betty felt that Ellen herself had not married well. Overcoming Ellen's long personal antagonism was critical in Ed's coming to any agreement with his sister.

Cutler was well aware of this problem. As a lawyer without any previous relationship to Ellen, he was in the best position to move her toward a deal. But Ellen kept switching gears—from wanting long-term control of the league with Jim to a quick cash settlement.

Cutler was shrewd and patient. Although he dealt with Ellen's lawyers most of the time, she said he was free to phone her and he did so when it seemed appropriate. He mentioned a precedent case in which a California wine family took years to settle their differences. She seemed less volatile after absorbing the implications of that. Toward the close of the bargaining with Cutler, Ellen dropped her threat of a court suit and requested that Ed sell some of the league's papers to pay her off in full. Ed would not agree. He and Betty had worked too hard to select his papers, and the league was growing more successful financially. Finally, Ellen agreed to sell her one-third ownership of the company to Ed for nearly $30 million. She was to receive the sum through a series of notes over a ten-year period. The arrangement required Ed and the league to go heavily into debt. Ed thought Ellen's price was a stickup but, after much cajoling by Cutler, agreed to the deal. Ellen thought that she had won a major victory. Ed was at first inclined to agree with her. Ellen was wrong. The newspaper business entered a period of very high earnings in the early 1980s and, after the ten-year period, Ellen's stock was worth almost twice what Ed paid for it. He and Betty now owned 100 percent of the company's voting stock. They gave their sons and grandchildren substantial nonvoting stock. The couple were, in 1978, for the first time since their marriage in 1950, complete masters of their fate.

Ellen now spends most of her time, with the help of a daughter, breeding spotted American saddlebred horses in Southern California. She is also active in the San Diego County Humane Society. Like Jim, once the deal was complete, she never spoke to Ed again. Old E.W.'s tradition of family fighting and division had prevailed.

Ed now recalls that in 1969, when he was running a two-ring news circus with Hagadone and Swift, the league balance sheet showed a great deal of debt, much less income and little cash on hand. By contrast, today the company has virtually no debt, has income five times as great as in 1969, and is loaded with cash. Ed's assessment of Betty's business astuteness had been borne out with the years.

League staff members felt that perhaps Ed and Betty would somehow break with the past and create a new and better future not only for themselves but their newspapers. The papers, with more than 1,500 employees and several hundred part-time workers, also were members of the Scripps family. These men and women had their own hopes and dreams. Fighting could only crush those aspirations. They felt it was time for a change. Ed pledged:

"We must surpass ourselves."

CHAPTER

7

FROM SADDLEBAGS TO SATELLITES

Community journalism is the cornerstone of all news practice in America. The nation's media giants—from wire services, metropolitan newspapers, and magazines to television and radio networks—trace their origins to the country's first small, struggling newspapers. Whether these were broadsides pasted on the walls of Boston public buildings and warehouses, land sales and business opportunities printed in the back rooms of Virginia general stores, or weeklies carried across the country in the saddlebags of Pony Express riders, news was born in grassroots America.

More than a century ago, E.W. Scripps and the nation's first media barons took the next logical step. They launched large news organizations—wire services, newspaper chains in big cities across the continent, and national magazines that served millions of readers. This expansion has increased even more with the emergence

Ed at work at Eagle
Hill, 1992

and upsurge of network and cable television companies of international dimension.

In recent times, however, some developments in the news business have been regressive and harmful. Many major newspapers have died or merged, leading to monopolies in scores of big cities. Even more recently, reporters and editors have created distrust among readers that newspapers may be biased and unfair. A "star" system, akin to that of Hollywood, also has arisen among large news organizations. Reporters on newspapers, magazines, and TV networks have assumed an importance—and entertainment value—sometimes as large as the stories which they cover. That is not true of most newsmen and women, but the practice is so widespread that it has tainted the craft. Nevertheless, large newspapers and magazines—TV to a much lesser extent—continue to be informative, interesting, and innovative. The higher salaries, promise of fame and glamour of the craft continue to attract "the best and the brightest."

If more money and prestige are to be found in large or national news organizations, why did Ed and Betty Scripps choose to build a company founded on small-town journalism? Who are the men and women who work for them? Why did they choose community careers?

Ed does not believe that more money is to be earned by owning and editing large newspapers. In fact, through community journalism, he has made more money than his cousin, Charles Scripps, the chairman of the E.W. Scripps Company. Ed Scripps's League of Newspapers is estimated to be worth more than $200 million. Charles Scripps's stock in the E.W. Scripps Company and other assets are valued at much less. The assets of all Bob Scripps's other descendants, who inherited the company from grandfather Scripps, also are estimated at less than Ed's—despite Ed's split with his brother. If E.W. believed he was punishing his son Jim's family by dropping them from his trust, he was wrong. They have risen like the proverbial phoenix from his ashes.

In 1950, with the flight of longtime residents from large cities, Ed saw not only the emergence of suburban newspapers, but more precisely, the growth of papers in small towns some distance from large cities. He took that straightforward concept of buying papers in nonmetropolitan areas and parlayed it over the years into the twenty-five paid-circulation newspapers, including eighteen dailies, twenty-three shoppers (free) and other publications that now compose the Scripps League. Their total circulation amounts to about 650,000.

The paid-circulation papers, with some 220,000 subscribers, are: *Argus Courier* in Petaluma, California; Arizona *Daily Sun* in Flagstaff, Arizona; *Daily Chronicle* in DeKalb, Illinois; *Daily Herald* in Provo, Utah; *Daily Journal* in Flat River, Missouri; *Daily Midway Driller* in Taft, California; *Daily News* in Rhineland, Wisconsin; the *Garden Island* in Kauai, Hawaii; Hanford *Sentinel* in Hanford, California; Haverhill *Gazette* in Haverhill, Massachusetts; Hazard *Her-*

ald Voice in Hazard, Kentucky; the Napa Valley *Register* in Napa, California; Newport *Daily Express* in Newport, Vermont; Novato *Advance* in Novato, California; *Ravalli Republic* in Hamilton, Montana; *Record Gazette* in Banning, California; Santa Maria *Times* in Santa Maria, California; The Dalles *Chronicle* in The Dalles, Oregon; *The World* in Coos Bay, Oregon; and the *Waikiki Beach Press* in Honolulu, Hawaii. The *Beach Press* is published in Japanese and distributed in Tokyo, Japan.

The twenty-three shoppers, which consist mostly of paid advertising, are located in the same cities as the paid-circulation papers. Their circulation amounts to about 430,000. The league also publishes *Appellation* magazine, which is produced in the Napa wine country and distributed in London, England.

The men and women who work for the company are a cross section of America. They work for less pay than most of their big-city colleagues in similar posts and perhaps with less glamour. Yet fame is relative. Most, if not all, small-town reporters and editors are personally better known in their communities than their big-city counterparts. Their firing lines are in the grocery and drugstore lines down the street where most folks know and meet them face to face every week. The league's newspapers, reporters and editors are typical of grassroots journalism throughout the country. The stories of these papers, their men and women, are a chronicle of modern community publishing.

More than 100,000 people live in the area of Provo and its sister city of Orem, Utah. The *Daily Herald*, flagship of the Scripps League, is published there. Mormons represent about ninety-five percent of the local population, the greatest per capita concentration of members of the Church of Jesus Christ of Latter-day Saints in the United States and the world.

Provo is also the site of Brigham Young University, an academically advanced institution with a reputation for scholastic integrity and discipline. The university has attracted not only many students who are not members of the church, but a sizeable foreign contingent. More and more computer companies are moving into

The *Daily Herald* in Provo, Utah, is the flagship of the Scripps League.

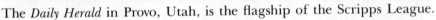

the Provo-Orem area, and the environs are gradually becoming a power base in the national computer industry. More than twenty foreign languages are spoken on the streets of Provo.

The university also has a top athletic program and keeps Provo in national sports headlines. Graduates include such stars as quarterback Jim McMahon, who played for the Chicago Bears and Philadelphia Eagles in the National Football League, and Danny Ainge who has been an outstanding guard for the Boston Celtics, Portland Trailblazers and Phoenix Suns in the National Basketball Association. Dozens of others have gone on to play pro sports.

Local LDS leaders in Provo-Orem, well aware that Salt Lake City Mormons are only fifty percent of that population, see themselves as the "last bastion of our church—the true believers." The Utah valley never attracted non-Mormons. Many locals trace their lineage to those pioneers who crossed the plains with Brigham Young and other church founders.

The *Herald* covers twenty-seven communities in Utah County, which is fifty miles north to south. It is published seven days a week. The newspaper has twenty-three editorial employees. The Utah County *Journal*, a twice-weekly paper, is its chief competitor.

Perhaps no news story in the past fifteen years has more clearly reflected the contrast between the people of Provo and the outside world than the Gary Gilmore case. In 1976, Gilmore, who lived in Provo and was well known there, shot and killed two young men during a pair of robberies in the city area. Gilmore, who had already served twelve years in prison for other crimes, was found guilty. He requested to be executed by firing squad. His insistence on the firing-squad sentence caused an uproar in the media and across the country. The American Civil Liberties Union appealed the verdict to the U.S. Supreme Court in a test of the death penalty. The high court upheld the sentence, although the ACLU fought it until the day before Gilmore died. Gilmore was executed by firing squad on a cold, snowswept January 17, 1977, at Utah State Prison. Author Norman Mailer wrote a best-selling book about the case, *The Executioner's Song*, which was later made into a movie.

Kirk Parkinson, publisher of the *Daily Herald*, was with the newspaper at the time of the trial and subsequent furor. He is the paper's third publisher in the past fifty years. The tall newsman is a native of Utah and a Mormon. His predecessors, Byron Jensen and Jack Tackett, were not particularly religious men but managed to fit well into the community. Tackett smoked big cigars and drank whiskey with gusto but had many Mormon friends who accepted him for what he was—a good man in the news business.

Parkinson, an affable man who has worked on the paper for almost twenty years, recalls the Gilmore uproar: "We reported the trial and its aftermath as we would have covered any such case. Other papers and the media, which knew much less about what was

happening than we did, gave the story much more space and sensa-
tionalized it in the process. The reason that we didn't publish all we
learned from Gilmore's friends and others was, the greater detail we
reported, the more our readers complained. They wrote letters and
stopped many of us on the street saying that reporting the case was
a disservice to the community. Provo was not a town of crime and
hate. It was a good, honorable community and we were destroying
its reputation. They concluded that nothing good could come from
reporting crime."

Local Mormons insisted that publishing the Gilmore murder
story not only was inconsistent with their faith but it created a guilt
complex among them. One man told Parkinson:

"I wish I didn't know about Gary Gilmore. I wish the *Daily Herald*
never told me."

The open-ended culture of America had clashed with the religious views of Provo's Mormons. Members do not challenge the
authority of the state, as those opposed to the death penalty had, or
the teachings of the Mormon church. In LDS, one avoids such
confrontation. The newspaper was being criticized for undermin-
ing the spiritual values of these church members.

The challenge of the *Daily Herald*, with its nearly 32,000 circulation, is still similar today: To publish a newspaper based on facts,
often unpleasant and sometimes even harsh, in a community that is
less receptive than almost any in the nation to crime reporting,
opposition to authority, and the permissive culture so widespread
across the rest of the country. Parkinson describes the community
with poignant eloquence:

"It's like living in a Norman Rockwell painting. Many people here
see the world in the narrow light of right and wrong. There are few
grays."

He recalls printing an AP story several years ago on changes in
LDS temple ordinances: "All hell broke loose. It caused real grief in
the community. We lost readers. LDS members said such rules were
secret and sacred. They were not to be discussed in public. Our
printing the story was viewed as sacrilegious."

Many people in Provo-Orem deny that teenage gangs exist in the area. They do and *Daily Herald* stories prove it but readers insist that no such groups roam the streets.

Earl Biederman is currently the managing editor of the *Daily Herald*. Unlike Parkinson and about ninety-nine percent of the paper's staff, Biederman is not a Mormon. In 1988, while still managing editor at an Oceanside, California, daily, he traveled through the Utah countryside on vacation and was struck by its rugged beauty. When the managing editor's slot at the *Daily Herald* opened late that year, he applied and got the job.

Biederman, a veteran newsman, insists that he edits the paper on the same basis as managing editors elsewhere in the country—he looks for what is significant and interesting to readers. The illness or death of a pope, for example, would undoubtedly be the paper's top story. If a famous American were murdered, that would probably make front-page news. The *Daily Herald* played the scandals of TV evangelists Jimmy Swaggart and Jim Bakker prominently. The paper also exposed local Mormons stealing $3 million from other LDS members in a health-center ripoff. But residents complained to the paper:

"We expect bad news in the world but not in the local newspaper. When there's trouble, we expect you to circle the wagons with us inside."

The five most important local interests are agriculture, computers, the university, the local steel mill, and Mormon church activities. Agriculture is the largest single industry.

N. LaVerl "Chris" Christensen was editor or managing editor of the *Herald* for thirty of his forty years with the paper. He served with the U.S. Navy in World War II. Typical of small-town journalism, his greatest scoop was not reported widely on the national scene, but to Provo it was an economic earthquake. The U.S. government decided to locate a 1,500-acre steel plant at the town's Vineyard Geneva Resort site. Christensen's story ran on February 8, 1942, in the midst of the U.S. military buildup during World War II. The story made some business pages around the country, but most Americans never heard of what was called Geneva Steel—or Provo, Utah, for that matter.

For more than forty years, the *Herald* reported every important development at the Geneva plant. It was to the newspaper and Provo-Orem what U.S. Steel was to Pittsburgh. Ten thousand workers were employed at the steel mill. But the *Herald* also reported that its dirty air and soot threatened the area's great natural beauty. U.S. Steel, which had taken over the operation from the government, eventually closed the Geneva plant. A new company, Basic Manufacturing and Technologies, reopened the works with a smaller but highly skilled work force. The company is now called Geneva Steel of Utah.

The people of Provo-Orem believe today that the plant represents a strong America. Mormons are highly patriotic and the nation's military and economic strength is important to them. Christensen retired in 1980 and died in 1989 at the age of seventy-five, but the *Herald* still covers the steel mill as extensively as when he was editor.

Compared to their parents of twenty or forty years ago, people of the valley still do not handle well the shades of gray involving many public issues. Answers or solutions are right or wrong. The issue of separation of church and state is more intense than anywhere else in the country. In the face of these views, Biederman maintains that his aim has never wavered: To put out a good newspaper that would be acceptable across the country as well as in the Utah Valley, while not trampling on anyone's religious convictions.

The *Herald*'s stated goal is a dicey proposition. One reason is because the virtually all-Mormon staff must make the transition from church member to reporter when they cover local government, politics and other issues. The man they are interviewing may be their church bishop. Reporters and editors say they can and do make the shift from church to the secular world, but the change is clearly not easy and is less than perfect. The newspaper rarely takes editorial stands on politics or religion but it regularly addresses the community's most important other issues. The *Herald* has often exposed political and other local corruption. The Provo-Orem area is overwhelmingly Republican and the *Herald*, like other league papers, chooses not to editorialize on politics except some local races. As Parkinson puts it:

"The area tends to be homogeneous. People don't like controversy or contentiousness. We inform the readers and let them make the choices. We editorialize when it's necessary for the common good."

Publisher Parkinson summed up working as a newsman in Provo: "Trust is very big here. So is betrayal."

More and more, the outside world is making secular inroads in Provo-Orem. Television, movies, music, and America's more liberal moral views have touched the lives of most local folk.

However, if the *Herald* is an example, it will take modern American society a long time to make a sizable penetration of Provo-Orem. *Herald* editors jokingly say the newspaper's greatest rival is the Mormon church, because its readers spend so many evenings in LDS work. The local religious commitment is extraordinary by modern measurements. As Parkinson said with a wry smile: "Our gross national product is kids. We have 3.5 children per family. Besides church and kids, there isn't a lot of time for outside activities."

Inside the *Daily Herald,* which covers 27 Utah communities. Now in its second century, it has a physical plant and printing facilities that rival any big city paper.

The *Herald* is now in its second century. Its physical plant and printing facilities rival any big city paper. It is more financially stable than at any time in its history. Some of its newsmen and women will never leave the paper—not for money, fame or glamour—because they view the lifestyle of Provo-Orem as superior to that of Broadway or Madison Avenue, Sunset Strip or Hollywood and Vine, Pennsylvania Avenue or Capitol Hill.

The Napa Valley *Register* is now 130 years old. Only three decades ago, the rich soil of Napa County lay mostly unplanted, although vineyards thrived in California as early as 1818. A new breed of settlers arrived in the late 1950s and early 1960s. They were determined to make the sweeping land of volcanic ash America's foremost wine country. They succeeded beyond their wildest dreams, establishing a multimillion-dollar industry. Today Napa Valley vintners compete with the best wines in the world.

Paul Donovan was one of those newsmen who would never leave community journalism. He worked in Napa, California, as a reporter, columnist, city editor and managing editor from 1936 until his retirement in 1972. He started on the *Register* in 1936 and later moved to the Napa *Journal*. Donovan returned to the *Register* in 1943 and was named Promotions Manager when the Scripps League bought the paper in 1958.

Donovan was a character. He loved good stories and large headlines. Perhaps his biggest claim to fame came in 1943 when he was on the *Register*'s wire service desk. War dispatches from the AP and UP reported that Allied troops, including General Mark Clark's U.S. Fifth Army, had reached the outskirts of Rome. Donovan got a map of the Italian capital and quickly realized that, from wire service descriptions, Allied tanks and infantry were close enough to enter the city within an hour, perhaps twenty to thirty minutes. The reports noted that the Americans and the other troops were still advancing. Donovan reasoned that, by the time the *Register* hit the streets, the Allies would be in Rome. He quickly rewrote the AP and UP and, under a wire services byline, put the Allies inside the

Eternal City. The *Register* blazed a banner front page headline that the Allies were in Rome. The story was a big scoop among Northern California papers. Rival editors in Vallejo and elsewhere screamed bloody murder because they were beaten on one of the biggest stories of the war. Donovan never came down to earth from that one. For the rest of his career, he was a man to be reckoned with.

Donovan tried to talk *Register* editors into all types of unusual stories in later years and often succeeded. His most lamented failure involved Bigfoot. He wanted to do a detailed story on the life and habits of the legendary man-animal that had been reported stalking the Northwest. Editors felt such a yarn would give too much credence to the woodsmen's tale and it might frighten children. Donovan kept trying over the years, but failed to convince the *Register's* brass. It was his one lament in a long and colorful career. Donovan passed away in 1990.

Three men lead the *Register* today—publisher Rich Heintz, editor Doug Ernst, and regional vice president Jack Morgan. Morgan, who has been with the league for nearly thirty-five years, actually supervises eight of its Western newspapers, including the *Register* and The *Garden Island* in Kauai, Hawaii. Each has his own views of community journalism and Napa itself.

Ernst is a thirty-eight-year-old San Franciscan, a graduate of San Jose State, who came to the *Register* in 1978 and became its editor four years ago. He says: "Scripps is family owned and warmer than a corporation. I wanted to work for a family-owned newspaper."

Ernst has a staff of twenty-two. His primary goal is to cover Napa County better for the paper's 21,000 circulation. The county has a population of 110,000, including 65,000 in the city itself.

The area is politically conservative. The region is flooded every ten to twenty years but residents will not vote to approve local funds for flood control. After its massive flood in 1986, voters refused to approve a twenty-dollar tax to clear the creeks of rubbish.

One issue has dominated Napa politics for the past quarter-century: land. A fierce battle has been waged between agricultural preservationists, grape growers and vintners, and real estate developers. In 1969 county officials decided that much of the valley was a national treasure and should be preserved. The county enacted an agricultural preservation law that forbade division of the land below a forty-acre minimum. Local leaders said Napa did not wish to become another condo jungle like Santa Clara County. New commercial and residential complexes rose against the open sky and began to stretch the limits of such cities as Napa, Calistoga, Yountville and St. Helena. Napa's county supervisors had switched back and forth between growth and no-growth policies. Urban voters, who controlled local elections, were caught in a Catch-22. They needed more room to grow but would diminish their quality of life—clean air and sky as well as rural charm—by every asphalt mile of expansion. Meantime, Napa County's environmentalists came to be as well organized as those in nearby Marin County near San Francisco.

A third of Napa's work force, mostly blue-collar employees, commute to jobs at Travis Air Force Base or the shipyards of Mare Island. To many of them, the vineyards on the hillsides are only a beautiful photograph in the distance—not a job opportunity to put money in their pockets. Large corporations, which own big sections of land, have relatively little commitment to the valley's future. Some have bought into the wine industry but could pull out quickly if profits nose-dived. The struggle between growth and no-growth groups is wide open and could change with the winds of fortune. The controversy continues today, with the *Register* in the midst of the conflict.

The newspaper, traditionally Republican, has favored slow growth. It prides itself on being out in front, not reacting to community developments. Heintz says: "Our challenge is to be on the leading edge of local issues. We're an aggressive newspaper. Our leaders are sometimes asleep. We're ombudsmen for what's right for the community. And we don't let the politicians sweep things under the rug."

The *Register*'s readers today expect the paper to take an active role in leading the community. They view it as not merely involved in checks and balances but as an organ of new ideas.

Heintz and Ernst say that, when they leave work for home in the evening, they want to feel that they have made a difference in the community. Ernst says: "We're as good as any metropolitan paper. Our people work hard, and believe in the product. Who wants to live in New York City? Our people fall in love with this area. Some don't want to go to a bigger paper, although we can't pay as much as a large daily. But we have other compensations."

Heintz adds: "Parents can raise a family here in a healthy, safe environment. The air is clean and the social environment is clean. There is little crime here. That is why we stay."

Heintz, who has been publisher of the *Register* for the past three years, became disillusioned with journalism in 1976. He saw a reporter on another newspaper fired because of a conflict between a news story and the paper's advertising department. He says: "If I couldn't find integrity in journalism, I planned to leave it. I needed to work on a paper with real integrity and told prospective employers that. Advertising and reporting should be like church and state—separate. The Scripps League was very concerned about ethics, so I began with the *Register*, after working on other papers, in 1976. I've been comfortable professionally ever since."

The publisher concluded with a laugh: "If we make a mistake, readers let us know fast—face to face. Reporters on big-city papers usually don't get that kind of feedback. The blessing and curse of grassroots journalism is, there is no hiding."

Jack Morgan, who loves the Napa Valley, does not drink wine. He's a Mormon. Yet the *Register* publishes more wine-industry news today than in its past. One page of every Sunday edition, for example, is devoted to a winery and its family. Morgan says there is no conflict between his beliefs and his job. Wine is simply a top local story. Morgan says: "I've never gotten any heat from my church—only my wife once in a while."

Morgan is working on publishing a league magazine about these wines, which will be distributed in London, England.

He spends most of his time meeting with the publishers and editors on the league papers that report to him. He is a kind of glue for these papers. Among them is The *Garden Island* in Kauai, Hawaii. The paper has a daily circulation of about 8,000, rising to some

21,500 with a midweek shopper included. There is a Sunday, but no Saturday, paper.

Kauai, the northernmost of the island chain, was the first of the Hawaiian islands to be discovered by Captain James Cook. It is called "the garden island" because of its lush terrain and breathtaking scenery. The island summit of Mount Waialeale is the wettest spot in the United States and in the world, with rainfall averaging nearly 490 inches a year.

Despite being viewed by tourists as an American paradise, Kauai's 52,000 residents have been battered twice in the past decade by devastating hurricanes. They also have been swamped by three tidal waves since 1945.

Hurricane Iwa struck the island in November of 1982, ripping apart homes, businesses, roads, communications and electrical power. Damage was estimated at more than $500 million. About 525 homes were destroyed, while nearly 1,450 others suffered major damage. Road, crop and other damages were very extensive.

The islanders were frantic for news—about the extent of damages, federal assistance, relatives and friends, insurance claims and other interests. Five members of the editorial and operations staffs, after picking up stories and photos from reporters and a photographer, flew to Oahu, where they put together a special issue at the league's *Waikiki Beach Press* on Thanksgiving Day—indeed an ironic twist. They flew back to Kauai with thousands of papers and distributed them free throughout the island. The thirty-two-page edition, filled with dramatic photos of Iwa's aftermath, is considered a historic document of island life.

Hurricane Iniki, the worst storm to hit Hawaii this century, steamrollered across thirty-mile-wide Kauai on September 12, 1992. Damage was estimated at $1 billion. One-hundred-sixty-mile-an-hour winds destroyed or damaged nearly half of the island's 21,000 homes. Some 8,000 people were left homeless. The storm killed two people on Kauai, one on Oahu, and injured more than 100. Public services on Kauai were knocked out for a week in some areas and much longer in others, including roads, water, electricity, telephones, and other necessities. Millions of dollars in crops, including pineapples, sugar cane and macadamia nuts, were ruined. Large sections of the island's beachfront hotels, basic to its large tourist industry, were washed away or badly damaged. An entire block was wiped out in Lihue, the principal city. Yachts were piled atop one another in nearby Port Allen harbor.

The catastrophe was again ironic for *The Garden Island*. It was celebrating its ninetieth birthday when Iniki smashed ashore. The plant's brick walls withstood most of the onslaught but, with no electrical power, the newspaper was unable to print its dramatic stories and photos. Instead, they were flown to the league's *Waikiki Beach Press* plant in Honolulu, and the first papers were airlifted back to Kauai for distribution on September 15. The paper, whose normal daily circulation was about 7,500, was distributed free. For days, however, it could not reach parts of the island because many roads were impassable and there was a lack of gasoline.

League headquarters in Virginia sent reporters cellular phones and laptop computers, since the paper's electricity remained out. While reporters and others kept working, all had suffered damage to their homes. Several had been totally destroyed. League staffers had rolls of tarp and plastic sheeting flown to the island for home-less employees. The staff ate their evening meals at a Salvation Army tent. Ed and Betty Scripps created a league fund at the Bank of Hawaii on Kauai to help their employees. The Scrippses, unwilling to take any bows for their contribution, would only admit that it was "substantial." Staffers on other League papers joined to make charitable contributions to the *Garden Island* Em-ployees Disaster Relief Fund. The paper said in a front-page edi-torial:

"Rebuilding Kauai will take time but it WILL HAPPEN. The aloha spirit of the Garden Island will not die!

". . . We will rebuild our lives, homes, businesses and community. Nature will heal many of the scars inflicted on the physical beauty of our island . . . the greatest source of pride we will have is the fact that, in the face of great adversity and human suffering, we stood together as friends and a community. May God bless us all."

Operations at the paper began to get back to normal about two weeks after the hurricane hit. The *Garden Island* provided free classified ads for islanders who wanted to let family and friends know where they were and how they were surviving.

The history of the paper, which the Scripps League purchased in 1966, is as colorful as probably any community paper in America. It was founded in 1902 by Somentaro Sheba, the son of an immigrant Japanese family. Some readers described the paper as looking like a "mimeographed sheet." A Honolulu newspaper said that the early issues appeared to have been "printed on a cider press, with shoe blackening for ink and carpet tacks for type." There were both English- and Japanese-language editions. The paper's twelfth issue featured local babies, a Republican political celebration, cattle and other livestock, and reports of various illnesses—all in complete disarray. Readers could pay for the paper with U.S. postage stamps.

The paper was printed in a cottage and later in a Lihue hotel which burned down. It was moved to a family carriage house which is now a store. In 1922 an impertinent young upstart named Charles J. Fern, who had been working on a local plantation, walked into the paper's latest plant near a highway and told editor Kenneth C. Hopper that he had a "lousy" sports section. Hopper immediately hired him as sports editor. Fern not only wrote about sports, he organized them—launching baseball and football leagues. The young man, the first pilot to land a plane on Kauai, later became editor, then bought the paper and became publisher. After forty-one years with the *Garden Island*, Charles Fern sold it to the Scripps league in 1963. Now one-hundred-one years old, he lives in retirement in Honolulu.

John Uyeno, who started at the paper as a janitor at the age of fourteen, worked his way up to become its publisher in 1971. This third-generation Japanese-American began at the *Garden Island* by answering an ad on a high-school bulletin board in Sacramento, California. He came to Kauai because he needed the job and had relatives on the island. When Uyeno began sweeping out and cleaning the place, the paper was located in a garage. He was not interned during World War II because the newspaper was taken over by the U.S. military and he worked for the Army. Uyeno also printed a military newspaper. He served as a military messenger and informal interpreter as well. John's most lasting memory of those days was: "I met a U.S. Marine who never drank water—only beer. I've never forgotten him. As a result, I take a beer now and then myself."

Uyeno was deeply moved when he was named publisher. The son of a carpenter, he came to Kauai as a virtually penniless teenager and rose to prominence despite the social effects of World War II. He was the first Japanese to become a publisher of an American-owned newspaper in Hawaii and perhaps in the United States. Uyeno, a smiling, affable man, is married with one daughter. He is one of the best known and most popular figures on the island. When Uyeno retired from the *Garden Island* in 1992, after more than a half-century with the paper, he turned over his publisher's chair to another Japanese-American, Edith Tanimoto. She too had worked her way up at the paper.

Tanimoto joined the *Garden Island* in 1961 after graduating in accounting from a local community college. Edith began as a secretary and bookkeeper. She was extremely adept in financial matters, including advertising revenues, and was promoted to head various departments. Born and reared on Kauai, Edith has one daughter and two grandchildren. She is among the first women publishers in Hawaii and the United States. She operates with a staff of forty-two employees. As in Uyeno's case, almost everyone on the island knows Tanimoto. She too has a winning personality, exceptional personal grace, and manages to charm most of the people that she meets.

The *Garden Island* is respected on Kauai and has political clout although it is independent politically. The biggest issue on the island is how much growth to permit.

Despite the fact that many investors from Japan have bought property and businesses on Kauai and the other Hawaiian islands and causing serious misgivings among many Americans—Uyeno and Tanimoto say they have no problems as Japanese-Americans. Indeed, the big spenders from Tokyo and elsewhere in Japan have lost hundreds of millions of dollars on their Hawaiian investments. Both John and Edith are viewed as native Hawaiians. The island, incidentally, now has more intermarriages between those of Asian and other descents than ever before.

The Arizona *Daily Sun* has long passed the century mark and is now the second-oldest, continuously operated business in Flagstaff. The Santa Fe railroad, which still rolls through the center of town, is older. Flagstaff has a population of about 45,000. It is famous as the home of Northern Arizona University, with some 15,000 students, and the Lowell Observatory, whose astronomers discovered the planet Pluto in 1930. They also have conducted extensive studies of Mars.

The newspaper was launched as the Arizona *Champion* in 1883 at Peach Springs, some sixty miles west on the Hualapai Indian reservation, but it moved to Flagstaff a year later. The first white child

Managing editor Mike Patrick (foreground) and weekend editor Leon Keith (background) at the *Arizona Daily Sun* in Flagstaff.

born in Flagstaff arrived only three years earlier. This was Indian territory, mostly Navajos and Hopi. The paper was named the *Daily Sun* in 1946. Ed Scripps bought the paper in 1957.

Platt Cline, longtime editor and publisher, owns twenty-five percent of the publication. Cline, a talkative and sometimes feisty man, began his career in 1938 at the Coconino (Arizona County) *Sun* as a reporter-photographer-salesman. Now retired but still writing historical books about Flagstaff, Cline, eighty-two years old, is perhaps the best known and most highly respected newsman in the state. The Cline Library at Northern Arizona University in Flagstaff is dedicated to Platt and his wife. Cline and Scripps independently of one another adopted the same newspaper outlook many years ago: Serve the community.

Although retired, he still visits the newsroom and crackles with comments on local folk and issues. Cline tells hundreds of stories about the news business. One of his favorites involves Eddy Gilmore, veteran foreign correspondent and a one-time Moscow bureau chief of the AP.

Cline recalls sitting down with Gilmore in a London hotel. Eddy had become famous as an American newsman who fell in love with and married a Russian woman in the Stalin era of the 1950s. He later tried to get her an exit visa but Soviet authorities refused. They finally allowed her to leave with Gilmore after much U.S. pleading and an uproar in the international news media. Eddy suddenly turned to Cline and said: "Platt, you took the right road. It's a lot happier life in small-town journalism. You have roots. I envy you."

In the 1960s, Eddy decided to visit Cline in Flagstaff. The mayor proclaimed an Eddy Gilmore Day. Eddy never made it to Flagstaff or any other small town. He died a few days after the mayor's announcement.

Another one of Cline's stories involves his old friend Bob Eunson, also a veteran AP man. Eunson was a graduate of Northern Arizona University's journalism school and began his career on the Coconino *Sun* and the Holbrook (Arizona) *Tribune-News*. He became an AP foreign correspondent and later rose to the post of AP assistant general manager. Bob, who also has passed away, always wanted more quality time with his family, friends and neighbors. He had long maintained that small-town journalism was a richer life than a career on the run. The Eunson Award is now presented each year to NAU's outstanding journalism graduate.

Cline's recollection points up the fact that community newspapering has become more appealing to a growing number of editors and reporters. He remembers one former big-city newspaperman, William G. "Bill" Hoyt, who came to the *Daily Sun* from the New York *Herald-Tribune* in 1958 as managing editor.

"Bill was an ornery, troublemaking guy who cussed a lot," Cline recalls. "Several times, women reporters and other ladies on the staff came to me en masse and resigned. I'd hire them all back the next day. Bill would apologize. He'd then go to the Veterans of Foreign Wars bar next door and get tanked up and return just as cussed as ever. The ladies would quit; I'd rehire them, and Bill would apologize. But he was one helluva newsman and he loved Flagstaff. Bill never looked back at New York. He was happy here."

The *Daily Sun* is a seven-day-a-week paper with a daily circulation of about 13,500. It doesn't pretend to be a metropolitan paper and has no extensive coverage of national or international events. It's a hometown publication emphasizing local news. In discussing the future of community newspapers, managing editor Mike Patrick said:

"We've got to have less Watergate mentality. We do report crime and corruption, but the days of trying to dig up dirt through investigative reporting are over. The *Daily Sun* went through that phase and we spent, for example, hundreds of hours investigating allegations concerning safety issues at the Navajo Army Depot west of town.

"I have four full-time reporters. I would rather have them work on stories that I know have wide community interest—that serve the community. We want to report what the community needs to know rather than have a reporter spend six months on a story that may lead nowhere."

The *Daily Sun* endorses no political candidates, but it does have a lively editorial page. Patrick and publisher Don Rowley sometimes disagree on what the editorial should say. But they do agree on one thing: "We should take a stand on local issues."

Paul Sweitzer, the local columnist, has been with the paper for more than thirty-five years. He reminisced about the past:

"You can't really talk about any newspaper unless you remember the old days. I recall covering three or four stories in one day. In 1963, I drove from Flagstaff to Florence and interviewed Patrick McGee, a convicted murderer, in the death house at the state prison. Then, I drove to Phoenix and covered a session on deer-hunting at the state legislature. I then hopped in my car and returned to Florence, where I watched McGee's execution. I got a hotel room near the prison, wrote all the stories, and dictated them to Hoyt, who had been out all night drinking.

"I decided to have some fun with the managing editor. We had a society editor on the paper for what seemed a hundred years. Her name was Billie Yost. Billie wrote all the obituaries and started every one of them the same way:

" 'Funeral Services are pending for (name of the deceased) et cetera.' "

"Hoyt told me he was ready to take dictation on the McGee execution. I read him this lead:

" 'Funeral services are pending for Patrick McGee . . .' "

"I never got to finish the sentence. Hoyt exploded:

" 'You miserable S.O.B.! I ought to execute YOU!'

"By the time I got back to Flagstaff, I had driven about 300 miles with numerous stops. Hoyt and I had drinks and a lot of laughs over the McGee lead."

Sweitzer looks back on his early news colleagues: "We were a drinking crowd. Most of us went to a bar just about every night. It's not that way today. Perhaps some of us will go for a few beers one night a week—Friday evening after work. I tell the kids that the place has become an insurance office."

Sweitzer is no insurance salesman. He wears a Cincinnati Reds baseball cap to the office most days. Sweitzer says his mother was a Reds fan. He has followed in her footsteps. The oldtimer confesses he has seen the Reds play only three times. But the cap is his trademark—unless he is covering the mayor or another formal story when "I wear a shirt and tie." He has made one more concession to modern journalism—the columnist has given up drinking.

The *Daily Chronicle* in DeKalb, Illinois, is nearly 115 years old. It is a six-day-a-week paper—no Saturday edition—with some seventy employees and a circulation of about 10,700. The Scripps League purchased the paper in early 1969. The city has a population of some 35,000. Barbed wire was invented in DeKalb. It is the home of Northern Illinois University, which has 25,000 students. DeKalb County is heavily agricultural.

One of the paper's claims to fame is the fact that ABC sportscaster Brent Musberger was once on its sports staff. But many local leaders and residents are sharply critical of the *Daily Chronicle's* editorial content—or lack of it—as well as its layout and typographical quality—an unusual number of typos and other errors. The paper is often referred to as the *Daily Comical*. The *Midweek*, a

Inside the De Kalb *Daily Chronicle*.

competing weekly, is more highly regarded by many local news-paper readers.

Veteran managing editor Lloyd Pletsch says the *Daily Chronicle* has more emphasis on local news than most league newspapers. He explains that residents can get their national and international news from Chicago papers as well as the Rockford *Register-Star*.

Various local leaders say privately that the *Daily Chronicle* is not a "player" in the community. It often fails to lead or actively support local causes.

Many in the journalism school at the university also are sharply critical of the *Daily Chronicle*. They maintain that the paper is dull and poorly written. Some say that the college paper often scoops the *Chronicle*.

Pletsch's editorials are generally considered fair, but other editorials are often viewed as poorly written, badly researched and vindictive.

Roger Warkins, executive vice president of the league, is head-quartered in DeKalb. Hank Crockett is the publisher. Warkins manages the operations for nineteen of the league's papers. He is a native of DeKalb who began at the paper as a carrier. The executive has been with the league for nearly twenty-five years. He is well regarded in both the league and DeKalb.

Warkins travels about fifty percent of his time visiting various newspaper plants and executives. Locals say he should spend more time overseeing the *Chronicle*. The newspaper needs improvement as well as greater community confidence.

The Santa Maria *Times* has changed more in the past dozen years than it has in its first hundred. In keeping with the Space Age ambience at nearby Vandenberg Air Force Base and California's computer revolution, almost everything at the paper is done with computers and word-processing equipment. Each reporter sets his own stories as he composes them, with final decisions on type style, width, etc., in the hands of editors. Worldwide, national and regional stories are beamed to a satellite circling the globe 22,000

Santa Maria *Times*
publisher John
Shields (right) dis-
cusses an advertise-
ment with classified
sales manager Trish
Isom.

miles in space, then beamed back into memory banks of the *Times*'s
computers.

These stories end up as photographic prints, which are cut and
pasted to form pages. Offset printing plates are fashioned from
these, again using the latest technology of electrostatic fusion.

The result is that pressmen can hang a plate onto the press only
moments after editors choose their final stories for an edition.
Minutes later, the press begins turning to print about 21,000 daily
copies of the paper. The *Times* also has a Sunday edition. Considerable time and money are saved in the process. The newspaper
became part of the league in 1975 shortly after a new building of
aggregate-studded concrete was constructed.

Karen White has been covering the Santa Maria Valley as a reporter for nearly thirty years. She has witnessed most of the local
growth. The city, located north of Santa Barbara, has a population
of 61,000.

As with many small-town reporters, Karen's greatest story came
from a major incident elsewhere. On January 28, 1986, the Chal-
lenger space shuttle exploded over Florida. All seven of the crew

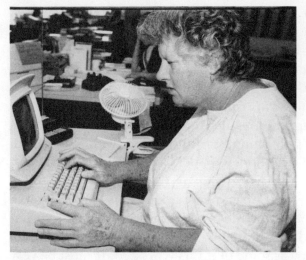

Reporter Karen White reviews a story on the Santa Monica *Times'* SII System 22. Karen has been with the *Times* more than 28 years.

were killed. Nearby Vandenberg Air Force Base had been selected as the West Coast launch site for future space-shuttle missions. The launching pad was already built. It would be a very big local news story and lift Santa Maria into national orbit as well. As Karen recalls:

"The explosion came in early morning Pacific Standard time. The paper had a noon press deadline. No one knew what to think at first. We were all in a state of shock. Then, because of all the publicity about Vandenberg and the next shuttle mission, we decided to get local reaction. My interviews with people on the street were devastating. They said the dream of a West Coast launching site was now out of the question. The program would be cut back as a result of the loss of life. The space shuttle program might survive but it would suffer endless delays and cost problems. It was like Santa Maria had died for twenty-four to forty-eight hours. As a city and a people, we just laid down and didn't move."

That was Karen's greatest story but not her most important. Her most significant has been her coverage of the county's growth—from sand, desert, ranches and farms to a population of more than 91,000. Some predict the population of Santa Maria will double within a decade. It's a mixture of farming, aerospace, a retail hub for the central California coast, service industries, and county government. The big local issue is agriculture versus urban growth. The *Times* has twenty-four full-time editorial staffers.

Publisher John Shields points out something that many people, including newsmen, do not always realize: "The competition here and elsewhere in small towns can be fierce. Wherever you look in community publishing, there is new competition. Much of this is attributed to desktop publishing, starting a paper with a very small amount of money. But distant newspapers, including major dailies, are trying to move in. Radio, television and cable are fighting us for the advertising dollar. Small-town newspapers must be good today. We've got to have not only wide-awake editorial and advertising staffs, but good production quality, including color. Community journalism is not sleepy as some of it was years ago. It must be very good to survive."

If the past is an indication, the League will survive for a long time.

The *Daily News* in Rhinelander, Wisconsin, celebrated its 100th birthday in 1992. Among its biggest stories were the Rhinelander Telephone Company changing to dial operation in 1956 and Richard M. Nixon visiting the city in 1968 while campaigning for the White House.

The *Record-Gazette* in Banning, California, celebrated its eighty-fifth anniversary in 1993. One of its biggest stories was typical of California history. A freeway was bulldozed through town in the 1950s.

The *Herald-Voice* in Hazard, Kentucky, with a daily circulation of over 5,000, is now more than eighty years old. The paper is well known for its local coverage from such hot spots as Big Creek and Viper. Judge Ray Corns writes the *Corn Crib* column.

The *Daily Journal* in Flat River, Missouri, is more than sixty years old but folks in town remember when the paper traded subscriptions for chickens, roasting ears of corn and other foodstuff. The paper started with "$25 down and the rest when you can catch us."

The Scripps League purchased the paper in 1973. It now operates with the latest computer and offset printing equipment.

In its nearly 350-year history, Haverhill, Massachusetts, has had eighty-four newspapers, among them the *Village Casket*, the *Agitator* and the *Ramrod*. Among the many stories that have appeared in the community's newspapers is this item of February 1804:

EPITAPH OF A SCOLD

> Beneath this stone a lump of clay
> Lies Annabelle Young
> Who on the 24th of May
> Began to hold her tongue.

The Haverhill *Gazette* was first published as a weekly in 1821. A subscription was two dollars a year.

The Scripps League opened a Washington bureau in 1978 to have its own independent source providing coverage of the nation's capital for its papers. The bureau chief and three reporters cover stories assigned by each of the papers as well as dig themselves for financial and other news that they believe will interest their editors and readers. Ed also wanted more offbeat news-feature stories from Washington.

Other league newspapers have similar histories, typical of community newspapers across the land. Their stories are the history of America. So too, in a different setting, is the history of Scripps-Howard.

CHAPTER

8

THE HOUSE
THAT E.W. BUILT

Scripps-Howard, a subsidiary of the E.W. Scripps Company, is the nation's ninth-largest newspaper publisher. It operates twenty-one daily newspapers in twelve states and Puerto Rico with a total circulation of 1.5 million. The company owns ten television stations, five radio stations, and cable television systems in ten states. The firm also runs United Media, the largest syndicator of newspaper features and comics in the world. The firm, with headquarters in Cincinnati, has about 10,000 employees.

The Scripps Company has operating revenues of about $1.3 billion a year. Its operating income runs some $188 million annually. Its net income has been between about $50 million and nearly $90 million in recent years. The national advertising slump beginning in 1989 has severely affected national media income. Scripps's net income had been about $90 million a year before the downturn.

Ed and Betty Scripps celebrate their 40th wedding anniversary at the Everglades Club in Palm Beach, January 1990.

The company has total assets of more than $1.7 billion.

This is the house that E.W. built. No one in the company claims to be his equal or successor—rather they are his inheritors. His beneficiaries. The crusty old autocrat has now assumed an aura of mystique, almost reverence, in company lore. The men who run the firm today are often viewed in America's media hierarchy as bean counters and bookkeepers. They are mostly faceless individuals with little of the intellectual challenge and editorial fire that characterized the old man.

Ed Scripps of the Scripps League looks at the company today and says privately that the Newhouse and Hearst corporations are better run and retain more of a traditional family spirit. However, he is reluctant to discuss the subject publicly. The crushing experience of his mother Josephine, with both the company and his once trusted uncle Bob, have left an indelible mark on his mind.

Bob's descendants comprise all the heirs of the family trust. The trust terminates on their deaths. Bob's twenty-eight grandchildren then inherit majority ownership of the company.

The trust's outcasts include E.W.'s six surviving grandchildren—Ed and his sister Ellen; three sons of E.W.'s daughter Nackey; and the great grandchild of John Paul. Company and trust chairman Charles Scripps is defensive about the outcasts. He said of Ed's father, who once had been E.W.'s prime heir:

"Jim was one of the most stubborn fellows I ever met but I loved him. He saw E.W.'s inefficiencies and made changes. I don't know who initiated the break between E.W. and Jim, but Jim was entrusted with an interest in newspapers that he took away. Whether one of the two was involved in a dirty deal, or who said what, I am not sure.

"Regarding Josephine's court suit, an unwritten family agreement entitled her to receive assets of the trust. Our company attorney, Newton Baker, argued that E.W. had the right to leave whatever estate he wished. The family accord should have had no (legal) bearing.

"It was an unfair decision to cut Jim off. But we were not there and had nothing to do with that decision. Therefore, for the trust, the question has no relevance. But I will say it has caused a gulf among the family."

He added: "That's true wherever there has been confrontation. It creates a 'We and Them' attitude. That makes for rivalry or jealousy."

Charles recalled attending a meeting of the American Newspaper Publishers Association. A Detroit *News* executive asked Charles if he had ever visited the paper. It seemed an odd question because he obviously had, so Charles asked the reason for the inquiry. The executive, referring to some members of Charles's own side of the family, confided: "No member of that branch of the family has ever darkened our door."

Charles was attempting to demonstrate that even within Bob's side of the Scripps family there were jealousies within jealousies and fights within fights.

Nevertheless, the chairman failed to explain his father's moral obligation to Josephine, who clearly had placed considerable personal trust in Robert. That is still a source of family friction. Charles says: "The feeling (of family division) remains with Ed and Betty. I do not feel it. I want to avoid conflicts of that sort."

Charles helped organize a Scripps family reunion in 1991 on the 200th anniversary of the family's arrival at Rushville, Illinois, its first home and E.W.'s birthplace. About 250 members gathered, some to meet for the first time, to celebrate the family. Ed could not go because he was still recovering from some heart problems, so Betty went alone, with some trepidation. Betty managed to speak with many of the family and had a pleasant time.

Charles may have wanted to heal some old wounds or simply to strengthen family bonds. Whatever his intention, the reunion was a success.

Betty's reaction to the occasion was more subdued: "It has been

Betty at the 1991 Scripps Family Reunion in Rushville, Ohio, with Susan Scripps Wood, younger daughter of Ed's brother Jim, and Susan's daughter.

very hard to understand that there is one side of a relationship that is business and another that is family. That seems to run through much of the Scripps family. Some simply do not trust the others. My husband feels that way very strongly.

"We have drifted apart—not only because of E.W.'s trust and Josephine's court case but we have different types of newspapers and principles. They have large newspapers and radio-TV operations which, for the most part, are located in big cities. We have community newspapers in small towns. We give our publishers and editors virtually complete freedom. They often dictate financial and editorial policies and decisions."

Betty pointed out, for example, that Scripps-Howard has published the booklet *We Submit*. Its prologue states:

"From this (E.W.) tradition has emerged the Statement of Policies and Principles, a formal blueprint to guide the concern's editorial writers as they confront today's matters of moment."

The statement then outlines Scripps-Howard's editorial guidelines on thirty different issues—from Africa to the nation's cities, from the national economy to education, from taxes and fiscal policy to welfare. The company says that its presidential endorsement is the only editorial which their newspapers must run. The papers matter of factly run editorials written in the Scripps Washington bureau. If a paper believes any one of these is inappropriate for their circulation area, they may phone Washington and explain their reasons.

Ed Scripps's editorial policy is contrary to Scripps-Howard's "editorial viewpoint on major issues." The league issues no guidelines or instructions to its editorial writers. Only one issue in the past forty years has caused Ed to break that rule. He suggested that his papers oppose the Panama Canal Treaty returning the canal to Panama. Some league papers assailed the plan but others took no stand. The Congress approved the treaty after a lengthy battle.

In terms of financial decisions, the league's publishers sink or swim on their own. If they ask Ed for advice, he may or may not offer it. As an administrator, he and his immediate staff are actually a service branch of the league. They provide for the papers' needs—from printing and computer help to assisting The *Garden Island* when the newspaper was hit with Hurricane Iniki.

Barry Scripps feels that Scripps-Howard ignores the League and pretends that it does not exist. That may be, but such a bias is understandable. The two are not in competition since they are in very different markets. The only thing they have in common is the name Scripps. Since Scripps-Howard is a much larger company, some executives and staffers may resent being confused or linked with a smaller firm. The point is objectively unimportant except that it reinforces the subjective division between the two companies.

Nevertheless, Ed has never expressed animosity toward his cousin, Scripps-Howard chairman Charles Scripps, although there is no close family bond between the two. They have met many times at national newspaper meetings over the years and had many friendly chats. Both have gone out of their way to introduce their wives to one another, but that is the closest that their relationship has ever been.

If Ed were to criticize any member of the company, it would be Roy Howard. Ed never trusted Howard despite the executive's long tenure with the Scripps organization. He felt that Howard not only made major managerial mistakes, including his running of UP, but played fast and loose as a man. Howard remained a strong influence at UP long after he left it for other company duties, and Ed held him in professional contempt for the wire's increasingly weak news coverage. Ed finally got so fed up with UP that the league papers quit it. Ed was completely turned off by Howard's personal flamboyance: "He finally had the name, the big office, the glory but he flunked out where it counted. He was a man big on personal prestige—not principle."

Charles Scripps returns the criticism but on another level: "Ed and Jim were young when they took control (of their mother's newspapers). I think that they got very bad advice. Sammy Hahn was their lawyer and he gave them bad advice. He bragged, 'I am able to do special things, do things that other lawyers go to jail for.'

Betty Scripps with
Jean Scripps, widow
of Charles Scripps's
younger brother Ted,
at the 1991 family re-
union.

We suspect that guy led them astray. They hit bottom but came
back."

Ed disputes this. He points out that the league had several lawyers, not just Hahn. He maintains that Hahn "was devoted to my
mother and never would have done anything to hurt her or us." The
newspapers which his mother took over were third-raters, not only
in the Scripps chain but in the cities where they were published.
Most had financial problems.

When all is said and done about the divided family, Ed says that
his parents' split with E.W. and the Scripps Company was a good
thing for three reasons:

—He has been completely free and independent to make his own
decisions throughout his long professional life. That was not true of
E.W.'s son Bob or Bob's son Charles—or all the others on their side
of the family.

—He has built his own company virtually from scratch. No one
in the Scripps Company has undertaken such a challenge. They
are executives of the firm because they were born into it. Most of
Bob's heirs have not grown up working in every department of the

newspaper business. They are inheritors—nothing more and nothing less.

—Ed has made more money than any one of them—on his own.

Ed sums up: "Nevertheless, there is no hostility between my cousin Charles and myself. We are on a very friendly basis."

Ed believes the Scripps Company made a major mistake when it went public a few years ago. In 1988–89, the company issued eight million shares of Class A common stock. These stockholders vote on one-third of the directors of the company. The offering, at an initial price of $16 a share, attracted more than $120 million—about $81 million going to the company and nearly $40 million to the trust.

The company has taken pains to point out that the public sale of EWSCO stock will not endanger the E.W. Scripps Trust's control of the organization. Ed Scripps believes that, if he could, his grandfather E.W. would rise from his watery grave off the African coast and start banging company heads together. Ed reasons that E.W. undertook his trust as an ironclad guarantee that the family would always control the company. Ed is convinced that going public inevitably weakens most companies, and this one in particular, because it has twenty-eight heirs with different objectives to satisfy. Nor do these great-grandchildren have the same sense of family tradition and loyalty as earlier generations. The league chairman maintains that meeting their hopes and demands will prove difficult, if not impossible, over time.

The company began selling stock to the public for precisely that reason. It took years before Charles Scripps, chairman of the trust for the past forty-five years, and other executives decided to do so. Charles is a quiet, experienced, often circumspect leader who does not always share his real thoughts. UPI was their albatross and had been losing millions of dollars a year for decades. The company did not want to fold the organization for two reasons—loyalty and a big immediate hit of at least $10 million in severance pay to employees. Finally, in 1982, the company practically gave away the wire service to a group of publishers and broadcasters.

The sale of UPI staunched the money hemorrhage, but it did not eliminate the potential for a major family fight. Some members of the family were already talking of selling their interest in the company to the highest bidder. That would mean litigation on all sides because the company insisted that other family members or the company had first rights to purchase any family stock. Others wanted company jobs for themselves, family and friends, and privately threatened trouble if their demands were not met. Other inheritors raised additional questions and problems.

The bruising battle among the Bingham family of Louisville, Kentucky, for control of its media empire sent shock waves through the Scripps family and other media dynasties. In one of the fiercest, bloodiest, public fights in media history, the Binghams were forced to break up their newspaper, radio and television organization precisely because a new generation demanded jobs, power and other prerogatives.

Scripps Company trustees believed they had no choice but to raise sufficient funds to buy out the squabblers. Unless they did so, some felt, several of the inheritors might sue the trustees claiming the officers had endangered the trust. The majority of the inheritors would probably have caused no problems, but the risk from others tipped the balance in favor of selling stock publicly. Betty Scripps has bought more than $4 million worth of the stock as an investment and because, she says, it is a good way to know what is going on in the Scripps Company. There is clearly a touch of irony—perhaps deliberate—connected with the purchase. Jim and Josephine's family again own part of E.W.'s firm.

To limit risk and enhance its control, the company purchased two million shares of Class A common stock from the Scripps family trust in 1990 at a cost of $31.5 million. That was $15.75 a share or twenty-five cents less per share than the first public offering. On completion of the sale, the trust owned seventy-six percent of the company's outstanding stock. The company's annual report pointed out the significance of the purchase: ". . . the Trust is required to retain stock sufficient to ensure control of the Company until termination of the Trust." Yet Ed Scripps still believes the company is vulnerable. He says: "Going public was a stupid thing to do, and it was against all of my grandfather's desires because he wanted to maintain the company's complete independence. There's no way that you can be truly independent if you're part of a stock company. You are always hearing footsteps or looking over your shoulder.

"The erosion of a company starts slowly, in small things. It's like taking a little dope—you gradually begin to lose control of yourself. One company heir will cause a problem here and another there. Suddenly, the company is in a crisis of conflicting views. You don't have to control a firm to create chaos, but once you do, the company often loses control. I am not speaking of today or tomorrow in the Scripps Company. This is going to happen over time. There will be one challenge and one court case after another. Running the company will become a nightmare. That's when things inevitably come apart and there is a change of command.

"My wife and I played the going-public game among ourselves. Eventually, we concluded, we would be fighting stockholders for control of the league. We would no longer be independent. That is very serious if, as E.W. wished, you want to own your own soul."

Ed Scripps maintains that the company should have found other ways to protect itself—even if they had to sell some of their assets.

When the trust expires, each male great-grandchild—E.W. allotted females only one-half share—will receive stock holdings ranging from a low estimate of about $20 million to a high of some $200 million. Each sum is based on a longevity formula that earmarks more money to those who live longest. Beyond that, no one is certain what may happen. For example, how quickly and how many heirs will sell their stock and skip? The present four grandchildren heirs—ranging in age from the late sixties to the mid-seventies—have no intention of upsetting the company applecart. However, their twenty-eight beneficiaries may have different interests, expectations, and aims. The extent and demands of those differences may well determine the Scripps Company's fate.

In a new bid to hold the company together, the E.W. Scripps Company and the John P. Scripps newspapers, which merged in 1986, have signed an agreement that will take effect after the trust's termination. The families are descended from two of E.W.'s sons.

The agreement will give signatories the first right to buy shares of

Betty with Louise
Scripps, wife of
Charles Scripps's
brother Sam.

the E.W. Scripps Company's voting stock when shares are offered
for sale by other signatories. The agreement includes provisions
governing the casting of common voting shares held by signatories.
For ten years after the trust ends, all common voting shares must be
subject to a majority ballot. The Scripps Company says that family
members who are likely to control more than sixty percent of the
outstanding common voting shares following termination of the
trust have signed the accord. The key word here is "likely." The fact
is, no one can predict what a good number of the twenty-eight
great-grandchildren of E.W. may do.

Meantime, chairman Charles says the firm is "turning more to
TV and cable for the future. We don't see many big papers for a
reasonable price on the market. The fact that we were in broadcasting during our lean days may have saved the company."

Asked for his views on E.W., Charles said: "He took ideas to the
limit to see where they would come out. He would have fought
today's establishment."

Indeed, he probably would have battled with both Charles and
Ed Scripps. E.W. was democratic. He fought with everyone.

9

PRIVATE PEOPLE

Ed Scripps appears happiest in his library at Eagle Hill. He and his wife Betty have traveled more than two million miles, but Ed says he has covered even more ground in his books. As a young man, Ed had been told by E.W. and others that he did not need a college degree to make a living but, if he were to be an educated man, he would have to read about 400 of the world's best books. Ed has done that—and more.

The ground-floor room is dominated by a painting of the cliffs of Dover, England, a gift purchased by Betty's parents on one of their many trips abroad. Replicas of the *Mayflower* and *Santa Maria* stand on the mantelpiece. An old walnut desk sits in the far right corner as one enters the room. From it, Ed can look out a window and see the Blue Ridge Mountains.

The bookshelves are full—Napoleon's *Memoirs*, the complete works of Thomas Jefferson, Carl Sandburg's *Abraham Lincoln*, the works of Browning, Santayana, Thackeray, Edward Gibbon's *The*

Ed and Betty Scripps on the occasion of their 42nd wedding anniversary at Eagle Hill.

Decline and Fall of the Roman Empire, the papers of U.S. presidents, especially Washington and Grant, the works of James Whitcomb Riley, Leonardo da Vinci, Washington Irving, John Greenleaf Whittier, *The Rise of the House of Rothschild* by Count Egon Caesar Corti, the works of Keats and Marco Polo, as well as books on music and the composers of the world's greatest operas.

　　Ed has two favorite books and has read them more often than the others in his library—Hervey Allen's *Anthony Adverse*, a novel commentary on early American life, and Oswald Spengler's *The Decline of the West*. The philosopher left an indelible mark on his native Germany and the rest of Europe in the first half of this century. Spengler dealt with the fundamental principles of existence. He was a pessimist along the order of the prophet Isaiah, whom he

Eagle Hill, the Scripps manor house, in Charlottesville, Virginia.

admired, but was often cheerful and witty. He detested materialistic humanists, utopians and pacifists. Spengler regarded person and destiny as interchangeable thoughts. He saw the polarity between the visible and invisible worlds—the spiritual destiny of individuals versus materialism—as much more important than the longtime tensions between East and West.

Ed says these two books have been the motivational forces of his life because of their depths of intelligence, spirituality and culture. For a lifetime, he has sought a better understanding of all three. These were precisely the goals of his grandfather. That is why E.W. suggested that Ed read the classics. E.W. still lives, despite their deep family differences, in Ed's thoughts and his library.

Prior to buying their farm in Charlottesville, Ed and Betty owned a beautiful two-story Mediterranean-style home in Hillsboro, California, near Betty's family home. Designed by the well-known architect John Warnecke, the house stood on three acres of land with a large swimming pool and tennis court. The Scrippses entertained there often. One of their more memorable dinner parties was for some 500 members of the Inter-American Press Association. Half of the guests spoke no English and the other half spoke no Spanish. The evening wound up being a night of charades. They also had a glamorous party for actress Merle Oberon and her husband, Mexican industrialist Bruno Pagliai. Will and Austine Hearst brought Bing Crosby, who stood at the front door saying he had not received an invitation. Betty coaxed him inside. Nevertheless, the Scrippses were not party people. They enjoyed their privacy more.

Betty is the practical, day to day, family organizer but friends see her as a visionary like Ed. She maintains a rigid schedule of business, exercise and meals. There are exceptions for family and friends, but the couple's regular regime is immediately resumed once these events have taken place.

The major reason for the rigid schedule is that Ed collapsed in the Scripps's winter home at Palm Beach, Florida, on January 1, 1991. He was rushed to Good Samaritan Hospital where he remained in intensive care for nine days. He was then moved by ambulance and plane to St. Mary's Hospital near the Mayo Clinic in Rochester, Minnesota. Betty was on the plane with him. Ed's heart condition was stabilized when a pacemaker was inserted in his chest. He was at Mayo for two weeks while his physicians attempted to trace the cause of his heart fibrillations and physical collapse, but his precise heart problems are still unclear. Betty stayed in a room near Ed during his entire hospital stay.

The horse barns at Eagle Hill, now used as an office.

The second reason is Betty herself. She is a fitness buff. Whether in Charlottesville or Palm Beach, the couple's day begins at 7:30 A.M. with a half-hour of laps in the family pool. The two then shower and dress. Ed is off again on a long walk with the family labrador Cocoa Bear. He returns to a breakfast at about 9:00 A.M. He and Betty share a light breakfast of a small orange or grapefruit juice, low-fat yogurt, toast, fruit, a small portion of cereal, and decaffeinated coffee, in the breakfast room overlooking the rose gardens.

The Scrippses had another yellow Labrador, Penny. She was considered an aristocrat among dogs, her Yarrow strain having won seven blue ribbons for obedience. However, when the Scrippses learned they would have to give her up for seven months during the training period for dog shows, they declined. Penny was a kind, gentle animal. When she died of cancer at nine years of age in the summer of 1992, the Scrippses were brokenhearted. They buried her on Eagle Hill Farm down by the stream where she had liked to swim. They held a family-only service for Penny, read a prayer, and placed flowers at her headstone.

Lunch and dinner are also light meals—vegetables, fish, poultry, salad, bread, cottage cheese and fruit. They eat steak or another meat about once a week. Betty has maintained a trim figure throughout her life and Ed has long slimmed down to 180 pounds.

After breakfast, Betty checks the house to see what work needs to be done. The couple has a small household staff. She also checks with the Eagle Hill management team to see what must be done on the farm. She then contacts the three-person staff at the league office across the grounds to see what news business, correspondence and other matters are pending. Betty consults Ed on the news agenda and follows up on their decisions. He normally reads after that.

The two have lunch at 12.30 P.M. and attend to the day's mail afterward in the library. This includes the regular delivery as well as overnight mail and fax messages from the league's administrative-service office near Dulles Airport at Herndon, Virginia, and the company's three vice presidents and General Manager stationed around the country. The two dictate answers to most of the correspondence immediately. It is then returned to the nearby league office, typed and mailed. Phone calls are sometimes necessary. Ed takes a nap and then goes to his office where he checks editorials and stories in league newspapers which arrive daily. Betty writes family and other personal letters in longhand. These include letters to organizations of which she and Ed are members.

Betty is a member of the board of trustees of the Thomas Jefferson Memorial Foundation, which owns and operates Monticello, near Charlottesville. Ed and Betty recently made an unrestricted $100,000 gift to the Jefferson Foundation. The organization is now leading the international commemoration of the 250th anniversary of Jefferson's birth. President Bill Clinton stopped at Monticello on his bus trip to his inauguration. He toured the enclave and then followed Jefferson's path to Washington.

The Edward W. and Betty Knight Scripps Foundation was created in 1987 and funded by the league as well as the couple. The Virginia corporation was chartered to make periodic donations to charitable organizations. Major gifts include those to the Mayo Foundation of Rochester, Minnesota—$750,000 thus far toward a goal of $1 million for the establishment of a professorship in medicine; the Scripps Clinic and Research Foundation of La Jolla, California; and the Palo Alto (California) Medical Research Foundation. Smaller contributions have been made to the American Red Cross of Washington, D.C.; the Palm Beach County Community Foundation; the Boys Club of Palm Beach County; and St. Mary's Hospital Foundation—all of West Palm Beach, Florida.

The Scripps League Newspapers Education and Research Fund was created in 1977. It has been funded by gifts of league stock and the income from three charitable trusts established by Ed and Betty. Yale University is the trustee of the fund which the New Haven, Connecticut, institution administers for the benefit of itself and seven other universities—Brigham Young, Northern Arizona, University of Arizona, Northern Illinois, Washington State, Hawaii, and the University of Virginia Medical School Foundation. Stock held by the fund was redeemed by the league in 1990 for principal and interest payments totalling nearly $5.3 million. Guaranteed annuities from the three charitable lead trusts total $180,000 a year through 1996. The purposes of the fund are to educate professional journalists and those coming up the newspaper management ladder as well as conducting medical research and scientific experimentation. The fund made income distributions of about $272,576 in 1992 divided equally among the eight universities. The league also has redeemed contributions to the Fred Hutchison Cancer Research Center and Pacific Northwest Research Foundation, both of Seattle, and contributed the vessel *Eagle Mar* to the Woods Hole Oceanographic Institution of Massachusetts. Ed and Betty also have made substantial private contributions to Episcopal churches in Virginia, Florida, and Lyford Cay in the Bahamas.

The Scrippses say they have allowed these contributions to be made public for one reason—to encourage other companies and families to do the same.

After Ed's review of his newspapers and Betty's correspondence, the two work or read—Betty likes biographies and business books—until 5:00 P.M. when both work out on indoor exercise bikes. This is followed by a shower and dinner in the dining room.

The two sometimes watch television—mostly news but also three entertainment programs—"Cheers"; "Murder, She Wrote"; and "MacGyver." Ed often listens to symphonic music or opera. He sometimes studies pending business or reads a book. On occasion, the couple spend the evening discussing business. Betty compiles the daily diary which she has been keeping since 1954. It contains nearly 500 pages of people, places and events.

Today, Betty is active with many luncheons, meetings and travel. The couple are very private people but this was not always so. In 1954, after joining the Inter-American Press Association, they traveled extensively in Latin America. The couple became members of IAPA to extend their intellectual, business and social understanding of journalism and international affairs. Both were inexorably drawn into the problems facing a free press amidst the hemisphere's military repression and dictators. They found that Latin American newspaper owners and editors were much more willing to discuss their fight for freedom and survival on a social basis rather than in formal meetings. Both wanted to help them.

Ed soon began assisting Latin publishers and editors. He became the top technical adviser to IAPA and later president of its technical center. He invited Latin members to tour his papers to learn the latest technological innovations in publishing. This help continued for years. Ed was elected to the association's board of directors.

Over time, on a confidential basis, Ed learned a great deal from the Latins—in particular the problems created by the South Americans themselves, since many of their newspapers are owned by large businesses and not individual news organizations. Ed valued his own professional and business independence even more. He also became more committed to freedom of the press in the United States as a result of implicit government threats and actual crackdowns on Latin newspapers.

The couple eventually bought one-half interest in a Costa Rican newspaper. They subsequently learned that their partner had privately sold part of his holdings to Robert Vesco, implicated in numerous Latin and other financial scandals. Ed sold his interest in the paper as soon as he could and never attempted to own a foreign paper again.

Ed and Betty share many memories from their forty or so trips to Latin America. They still remember their first trip to Rio de Janeiro in 1954, shortly after the loss of their baby. Actress Ginger Rogers happened to be there at the same time. The society page of the city's leading newspaper carried two big headlines: GINGER ROGERS IS IN TOWN and MRS. SCRIPPS CAUSES A SENSATION IN RIO. Betty's story featured her jewels, furs and clothes. The story lifted her sagging spirits.

In 1972, the Scrippses were visiting Costa Rica. Betty's picture appeared on the front page of the leading morning newspaper with other IAPA members, sharing a champagne toast with the president. On the following morning, Ed picked up the same paper whose headline was PRESIDENT SHOT BY PALACE GUARD.

The couple bought a retreat home at the Lyford Cay Club in

As members of the Inter-American Press Association, Ed and Betty traveled extensively in Latin America. In 1971, Betty shared a champagne toast with the President of El Salvador. The next day he was assassinated by his palace guard.

Nassau, the Bahamas. Founded by Eddie Taylor, a Canadian financier, the club attempted to bring together self-made men and their families with others of similar background. Ed says he met some of the most interesting people in his life among the club's membership.

At dinner there one evening with José Bosch, a Cuban-born businessman, Ed asked Bosch how he had come to the club. Bosch related that he had fled Cuba after Fidel Castro overthrew the Batista regime in 1959. While running to his boat in a bid to escape, he was shot in the leg by a Cuban soldier. Bleeding steadily, Bosch managed to pull himself aboard his vessel, start the engine, and set out for the first port available—Nassau.

Bosch eventually motored into Nassau and walked up to the desk clerk at the Nassau Beach Hotel. He still had the bullet in his leg and his pants and hands were saturated with blood. Bosch said to the stunned clerk: "I know that you don't know me and I look terrible.

I'm a Cuban businessman and have money but don't have any with me. If you'll give me a room, I'll see that the hotel is properly paid. And I'll take care of you for helping me out."

The clerk replied without hesitation: "Yes, we'll give you a place to stay, dress your wound and take care of you. Give me your name and here is your room key."

Bosch was so surprised and grateful that he eventually built a home on the grounds of the club and constructed a Bacardi rum plant on Nassau. He has been there ever since.

Betty remembers some of the parties at Lyford Cay with friends Lord Harmsworth of England and his wife, who recently passed away. Also Princess Bismarck, the widow of Prince Otto of Germany, as well as Lord Henry and Lady Colyton of England, and the Oakes family, owners of many islands in the Bahamas. In 1983, Betty became cochairwoman of the House Committee at the Lyford Cay Club. She shared these duties with Diana Barnard Schumacher, a longtime friend. The Scrippses eventually sold their home in Nassau when they cut down their traveling, but they still own four lots at Lyford Cay.

In 1980, the Scrippses attended when Prince Phillip awarded the Templeton Prize in Buckingham Palace to Professor Ralph W. Burhoe of Chicago. The international prize concerns a distinguished contribution to religion. They were invited by Lord and Lady Templeton, who lived at Lyford Cay. The Templetons knew of the Scrippses' interest in religion. Each year an international board of advisers chooses the individual in the world whom they believe has most helped to increase man's understanding and love of God. The award is an attempt to interest more people everywhere in religion.

The Templetons invited the Scrippses to London again in 1982 when they gave a large dinner for friends there. Betty sat next to Lord Hume, the former prime minister, and the Reverand Billy Graham. Lady Pindling, wife of the former prime minister of the Bahamas, was nearby. Betty later said that the conversation about world affairs was the most stimulating of her life.

The same year the Scrippses were aboard the initial run of the new Orient Express from London to Vienna. The Templetons and members of the British Royal family were aboard.

Betty recalls trips to Buenos Aires before and after the rise of strongman Juan Peron. The Argentine capital at first reminded her of Paris with its wide boulevards and stylish men and women. For a capital city, she says, it was a calm, lovely place to visit. After Peron took over, the trappings of military power became the country's style. A large photo of Peron and his wife Evita greeted everyone at the airport and spread to all parts of the city. The watchful eyes of armed troops on various thoroughfares could not be missed. Betty says the hotel concierge advised her one day not to go out on the street because crowds were in an ugly anti-Yankee mood after a Peron speech. He told Betty that, with her blonde hair and blue eyes, she would probably be in trouble. She never left the hotel except to go to IAPA meetings with Ed.

Betty met Jack Knight of the Knight-Ridder newspaper chain on these Latin trips. The two decided that they are probably related because both their fathers were born in neighboring West Virginia towns. Jack has nothing against a good-looking blonde in the family. He met Betty's father, Howard Knight, in 1959 in California and remarked that they looked alike.

Ed was the center of attention during their 1973 visit to Japan. The couple had their first Japanese sit-down dinner on the floor cushions of a Tokyo restaurant with a group of American friends. Ed had only one cup of saki, so he was sober. The long meal finally concluded, Ed tried to rise—and tried again. His six-feet-four inches and 250 pounds would not budge from his cushion. Two male waiters, then three more, attempted to assist him. No luck. Two others arrived, making it five helpers. Still not enough oomph. Two more arrived—a lucky seven—and after groans, moans, and a loud scream that sounded like "*Banzai!*", they lifted Ed from the floor. He tipped them generously and, as Ed puts it, he has never sat down on the floor for more than a minute or two ever since.

The Scrippses liked the international social life—they even spent seven summers on the French Riviera in the 1960s—but the two were always happy to come home.

In 1978, the couple moved from California to Eagle Hill in Virginia. They heard of the place, a farm for raising thoroughbred Arabian race horses, through Youka Troubetzkoy, a Russian prince, who lived on the French Riviera with his wife Marcia. Troubetzkoy, a gregarious world traveler, and his wife had become friends of the Scrippses. He had wed Marcia Stranahan, heir to the Champion spark plug fortune, in 1949. They were married until she died in 1974. Troubetzkoy had left the Soviet Union after his House of Romanov fell, and became an actor in Hollywood. The prince was a down-to-earth, humorous guy, who was a pal of Douglas Fairbanks, Cary Grant, Errol Flynn, Lucille Ball, Mary Martin, Vincent Price and other actors. He introduced Ed and Betty to Jimmy Lewis, Marcia's half brother, who was selling Eagle Hill. Ed fell in love with the place and bought it for $1.4 million.

Betty with Prince Youka Troubetzkoy, the gregarious Russian who introduced them to Eagle Hill, at Villa Olivula on the French Riviera, 1965.

Shortly after Ed and Betty moved to the farm, they were invited by neighbors, the John Rogans, to a lunch for President Gerald Ford. A heavy October snow blanketed the Virginia countryside the morning of the luncheon. They plowed through the drifts to the Rogans' where everyone, to their surprise, had shown up. This was not California—in weather or luncheons!

The decision to move had been a big one, since Ed and Betty were such longtime Californians. Ed wanted to be closer to the league's papers in the East and his Washington news bureau. One-third of the papers were in the East and no one was directly supervising them. Their two sons and other executives could oversee the Western papers. Neither has ever admitted it but both were becoming disenchanted with California. The state had become very crowded, hurly-burly, and the new crowd that had pushed to the top of the social ladder in San Francisco were often a pushy, rough-and-tumble group determined to set their own new agendas.

This was not Ed's or Betty's style—or substance. Betty was a member of the Daughters of the American Revolution and the Colonial Dames of America. The Scrippses are listed in both the New York and Palm Beach social registers. Their club and other memberships include the Villa Taverna Club, St. Francis Yacht Club in San Francisco; the Lyford Cay Club in Nassau; Framington Country Club and the Boar's Head Sports Club in Charlottesville; and the Bath and Tennis Club, the Everglades Club and Beach Club in Palm Beach as well as the Florida Surf Club, and the Colony Club in New York. Betty was also on the board of directors of Southeast Bank of Miami and St. Mary's Hospital in West Palm Beach Florida, a member of the Health Science Board of Directors at the University of Virginia Hospital, and the International Board of Scripps Clinic in La Jolla, California.

In 1992 Betty attended a dinner in the newly decorated Scripps Hall at the Scripps Institute of Oceanography in La Jolla, California. Barry and his wife, Gail, accompanied her. The dinner guests were solely members of the Scripps family from around the country.

Ed and Betty owned two private planes in the first twenty years of their marriage but no longer do so. Their organization has also owned various sea-going vessels. The latest is the eighty-six-foot *Betty Jeanne II*. It reflects Ed's contemporary outlook—the latest fax machines, computer satellite links, and other technology keeps him in contact with his newspapers.

The couple purchased a winter home, "Karnak," at Palm Beach in 1986. They spend five to six months a year there, from sometime in November until late April or the first of May.

In 1990, the league set up a new accounting and administrative-service headquarters in Herndon, Virginia, near Dulles airport. The company's legal, computer research and other departments were joined there. The move was a company milestone because its headquarters had always been located in the West.

Also that year, Ed and Betty celebrated their fortieth wedding

The *Eagle Mar*, the Scripps' yacht, which they donated to Woods Hole Ocean-ographic Institute as a research vessel.

anniversary at the Everglades Club in Palm Beach. About 135 family and friends came from around the country and the Bahamas. It was a lovely affair but there was one sad note. Betty was disappointed that her father was not present. He had died two years earlier in Palm Beach. Her mother, who is ninety-three, still resides in Manalapan, Florida. The two are extremely close.

Looking at Ed on that day, his friends said: He hasn't changed in the past four decades. Ed is still a man of values. His watchword is still freedom—of action, business and communication. And to ride his motorcycle a few more times. He won't surrender that hope.

Her friends' view of Betty: She's still the achiever. Apart from Ed, that's her fun in life—to accomplish something worthwhile. She's as persistent and determined as ever. She has become a newspaper woman.

It has often been said that behind every great Scripps man there has been a strong and determined woman. Patriarch E.W. had his influential older sister Ellen and his strong-willed wife, Nackie. His son Jim was supported in his darkest hours by his indomitable wife, Josephine Stedem Scripps. And Jim's son Ed has Betty. It is difficult, if not impossible, to say who was the strongest of the four women but it is certain that all have been formidable individuals.

Today, the Scrippses treasure friends around the country and in various parts of the world, but as in "September Song," Ed Scripps's world trips are dwindling down to a precious few. In the twilight at Eagle Hill, the couple now savor time, their children and grandchildren, old friends and places. Their work remains central to their lives. They are worth well over $200 million, but the couple's major concern is their good name, the good reputation of their newspapers—and how they will eventually bequeath their legacy.

It is indeed ironic that Ed and Betty must now respond to the same dilemma which faced E.W.—who would be the heirs of his newspapers and fortune? That decision, which banished them from E.W.'s empire, was the turn in the road from which the Scripps League began. Ed and Betty now face a similar crossroads.

10

GRASSROOTS

The local newspaper is the soul of a small town. It's the community's heartbeat and voice. The daily or weekly publication is more than the mirror of local life—birth, school, marriage, work and death. It is its very identity.

More than 1,100 communities across the country are served by daily newspapers with circulations of less than 25,000. These grassroots publications represent more than two-thirds of the nation's daily papers.

There are more than 7,400 weeklies in the United States. Most operate in small towns. Their paid and free circulation totals nearly fifty-five million.

Only with some comprehension of these measurements can one begin to understand the enormous influence of small-town papers. Most of them are much more credible than large metropolitan papers, other national publications, as well as network radio and television news. The simple reason is, most are home-grown products.

Ed with Lloyd N. Cut-
ler, aboard the *Betty
Jeanne II*. Cutler, a former advisor to
President Jimmy Car-
ter, saved the Scripps
dynasty from another
legal battle.

Various studies, including one by Colorado State University, offer
a profile of grassroots weeklies. Eighty percent of these papers serve
communities located more than twenty-five miles from population
areas of 50,000 or more. Only two percent are within five miles of
such cities. More than one-half of these papers are located in rural
or farm communities. Twenty-four percent are in commercial centers and nine percent are in suburban communities.

TV news representatives often boast that most Americans get
their news from television. That may be true in a superficial sense
but the claim is inaccurate on serious examination. Most Americans
still receive their daily intake of information from the printed
word—from newspapers and magazines to books and textbooks.

To further comprehend the importance of small-town papers, a
reader need only compare them to TV news coverage or, for that
matter, to large metro papers. Neither TV nor metro papers cover
small towns on a regular basis—from city and town council meetings to the struggles of the local school board. The biggies do not

report on most local business and industrial developments or virtually any civic, church or social clubs. Funerals, weddings and local feature stories also are completely ignored by the nearest TV Eyewitness News or metro daily. The biggest fish and tallest corn stories never see the light of day in the larger media. That is not surprising because metro readers, viewers and listeners could care less about what happens in Sleepy Hollow or Little Creek.

In most small towns, there is no local news except that in the paper printed on Main Street. Folks would rarely if ever know what was going on at the town hall, the justice of the peace or the local elementary school without old Mr. Jim or his young assistant coming around to ferret out what was happening thereabouts. This says nothing of Aunt Millie's Thursday night bowling score.

No institution in America has a finer record of public service than the small-town newspaper. It has forced more open and honest government, and has created finer schools, better health care, safer streets, and more recreational facilities than any other source in these communities. Many of these papers have helped lead the way toward racial equality and understanding, assistance for the poor and homeless, and a cleaner local environment. Few local charities could succeed without the free publicity they get in these smaller publications.

Small papers are powerful not because they are the only game in town but because they are truthful and engender trust. They also point the way to the future. Many folks have summed up their influence in local vernacular:

"They help keep the jailhouse dogs out of the mayor's seat."

Ed Scripps heard the song of small-town newspapering more than four decades ago in his mid-forties. His was a late vocation but his career could not have been based on a simpler inner calling— freedom. Ed was searching for greater professional and personal freedom. He wanted to call his own shots—not by influencing readers but by giving them the freedom, the forum, to make decisions so their communities would be better places to live. He also aimed to make a reasonable profit for his risk and avoid fierce big-city competition. Rural, small-town newspapering was a virtually perfect choice.

Across the country today, there is fear and criticism that newspaper chains are motivated more by maximizing profit than the well-being of the many communities which they serve. At the start of this century, slightly more than one percent of the country's daily papers were owned by chains. Five years ago, however, more than seventy percent of all dailies were owned by chains, from Gannett and Knight-Ridder to Newhouse and Scripps-Howard. Yet the growth of corporate ownership has been accompanied by a decline in per capita readership. There are many reasons for this slippage, such as newspaper content and design, but the most significant factor has been the inability of corporations to maintain good community ties.

Decades before many of his contemporaries, Ed Scripps committed his papers to community service. To maximize that service, it would be necessary to turn over virtually complete control of his papers to local staff and executives. These men and women would be directly responsible to their readers. In turn, they would encourage community involvement in the papers.

Ed is a trusting individual. He is known in the news business as a highly ethical professional. He has always avoided involvement with any special-interest groups. His colleagues report that Ed has constantly put principle ahead of business interests and truth before friendship. He has long been quick to point out when money, public or his own, was being spent unwisely. Ed also has always encouraged the development of good leadership—not only among his news staffs but in the communities where they are located. These observations define the strongest personal and professional characteristic of the man—honesty.

Despite the fact that Ed has extensive knowledge of high-tech newspaper machinery, he says: In trying to publish a good newspaper, trust your people, not your tools. He adds about readers:

"My basic philosophy for more than forty years has been that people are basically good. If people are given accurate, timely information, they will make good decisions. They will appreciate good news coverage and, as a result, circulation as well as advertising will grow. Unfortunately, and I am not trying to point fingers, this has not been the torch lighting the way for some newspapers. Many of them have spent more time on advertising and circulation rather than what readers most want to know. Circulation, advertising and readers' interests are interconnected. They must be seen and treated as such. All three are our bread and butter, meat and potatoes."

To a degree, some chains have adopted Ed's policies in recent years but many are still searching for other reasons to explain their declining per capita readership.

Ed hasn't stood still. In meetings with his editors and publishers,

Ed and Betty Scripps at a party honoring James S. Copley of the Copley Newspaper family. From left: John P. Scripps, Jim Scripps, unknown, Marian Scripps, James S. Copley, Betty Scripps, Ed.

he has long encouraged league papers to cover a wide span of interests—from advice to the lovelorn to health, gardening, cooking, diets, astrology, more sports and greater business coverage.

He has sought reporters and editors who genuinely cared about the towns which they covered. That is one reason why it isn't necessary, even these days, to hold a college degree to work on the news staff of any League paper. They often accept high-school graduates committed to their home towns rather than college men and women who view the papers as mere stepping stones in their careers.

Newspaper executives today are more critical than ever of college journalism courses. They maintain that professors are too aloof from working news people, their papers' problems and readers. The newsmen insist many teachers are not only insensitive to the latest issues confronting their papers, but have not associated themselves with the current movement to bring readers and reporters closer together. The goal of most papers today is to listen more and thus get closer to readers' lives and what they are thinking. Ultimately, papers aim to provide a forum for readers' views. The idea that an informed citizenry can govern itself is the basis of democracy.

Reporters can no longer merely raise hell in a series of articles or an exposé. They must offer solutions to readers' problems.

Most newspapers today, large and small, are taking one readership survey after another. They describe it as "listening to readers' interests." For example, the surveys ask what issues interest readers most. One overwhelming conclusion is that readers are frustrated with local, state and national government. Various newspapers have written a detailed series of articles about these frustrations. Additional series are planned. That is one answer to the increasing skepticism of readers about the press.

The same surveys clearly show that readers and listeners have lost confidence in the media and news profession. Some of the major reasons for this include advocacy journalism, irresponsible investigative reporting, and expressed or implied bias of newspapers and their staffs.

Ed condemns advocacy journalism in which reporters express

their personal views as factual information in news columns. He says it is the curse of journalism and will not permit it in his newspapers. Ed says, if that is interference in local control of league papers, so be it. Based on interviews with his editors and publishers, they agree with him—without prompting.

Despite claims by some reporters and editors to the contrary, Ed emphasizes that readers expect objective news coverage. This has been demonstrated in surveys and studies despite arguments by some alternative weeklies and others who are still attempting to justify playing loose with the truth. These editors argue that objective reporting is not attainable and use this false premise as an argument for advocacy reporting. Objective reporting does not mean infallible communication—a straw man set up to challenge the vulnerability of objectivity. Ed says it stands for as much truth as reporters and other humans can attain in pursuit of their profession.

Another reason for some readers' distrust of the media is the fact that a number of news people have openly taken sides in politics and on such issues as abortion in their reports. They argue that their jobs do not require them to surrender their First Amendment rights.

The American Society of Newspaper Editors, after much debate, finally issued this statement of ethics: Journalists should "neither accept anything nor pursue any activity that might compromise or seem to compromise their activity . . . Good faith with the reader is the foundation of good journalism."

The Associated Press Managing Editors Association said: "Even the appearance of obligation or conflict of interest should be avoided . . . Involvement in such things as politics . . . that could cause a conflict of interest, or the appearance of such conflict, should be avoided."

Reporters are observers, not participants. Ed says they abandon the trust of their readers when they become advocates of any cause. These newsmen still retain First Amendment rights in that they can vote and take any private position that they wish on such issues as abortion. The First Amendment was not written to protect editors and reporters but the public. Columnists, by definition, write their own opinions but they cannot falsify facts to support their views.

If newspapers are to capture more respect from their readers, they must interact with subscribers more than they do. One way to accomplish this is to form organizations like the Minnesota News Council, which was established more than twenty years ago. The council was composed of half media and half public representatives. It set up a review body to evaluate the public's complaints and to state the council's opinions of these readers' views. News executives in other states at first rejected such a council, but today most seem to favor it. The council sees itself more as a guard dog than a watchdog over the press. Its conclusions on public complaints are publicized but these judgments do not carry sanctions or penalties.

Some newsmen, claiming their professional responsibility and freedom are being invaded, still chafe at the idea of a news council. They seldom mention their major reason: They are as thin-skinned as their readers about being criticized in public. TV stations in Minnesota are voicing strong support and use the council. So are various newspapers around the country. The Minnesota body is now offering its services to papers outside the state. The time has come for such readership input but many papers are still dragging their feet. However, they will eventually catch up to the news.

Despite the reluctance of many to support the Minnesota council, most news executives now say that, first and foremost, newspapers must become more reader-involved. The press must be responsive not only to readers but the marketplace where the competition with other papers, magazines, radio and TV has become fierce. To do this, they must hire better staffs who are truly part of the communities in which they work. That sounds like Ed talking more than forty years ago.

These executives are alarmed because of a one-third plunge in newspaper readership over the past twenty-six years. In 1967 three out of every four Americans read a newspaper every day. Today only one in two reads a daily paper. Newspapers produce about sixty-three million copies a day, an increase of only 2.3 million copies over the past twenty-five years. But the number of the nation's households has exploded—soaring about fifty-six percent.

Editors admit that most papers have not kept pace with readers' interests—most aspects of the economy, including what America's international competitors are doing, the stock market and the job market of the future. Readers want more information on how to raise a family, ideas and costs for leisure-time activities, and health news—from diets to the best fitness programs.

To gain more readers, many newspaper editors and publishers have jumped on the "packaging" bandwagon. They want to look like *USA Today* with shorter stories, more graphics, greater color, and more compartmentalization. Despite making these changes, many papers are still falling in market share and penetration.

Traditional weeklies and smaller dailies have, for the most part, shunned "packaging." They aren't made flashier by running more graphics and color. Some aren't well designed or even written particularly well. Yet these papers continue to expand their readership. Why? To a large extent, the answer is local news coverage. These newsmen know that their paper is the single source of information for local readers. If they don't print a story, it will never appear anywhere. So they print it—from a list of students starting first grade to high-school seniors who have won university scholarships. They are the most powerful pieces in all of journalism because they involve family, friends and neighbors.

In a small town hardly anything is more sensitive than the editorial page in the local newspaper. In some ways, the most important part of that editorial page is the letters to the editor. That is because readers are actually participating in informing the public and expressing viewpoints that often oppose the paper's editorials and its columnists. They also call other readers' attention to subjects and views that have not appeared in the paper. It is the pure voice of the community, untouched by editors and reporters.

A newspaper can write the best editorials in the nation but, if it's not publishing diverse viewpoints and debate on local public issues, it is not fulfilling its social responsibility to its readers.

Betty Scripps with
William Randolph
Hearst, Jr.

The same can be said of letters to the editor, which first appeared in 1722. These letters are not merely to capture the "pulse" of the public but, as indicated, to offer alternative viewpoints on important issues. Majority opinion is not always right. New ideas can not only be better but change the course of local government, education and a host of public concerns. These letters reflect the real community, not a spoon-fed town that accepts ninety percent of what the mayor, local officials or newspapers say.

Readers are sometimes afraid to write these letters, since they might be held up to ridicule by the paper or others. The good newspaper will encourage such writing because new ideas can make a more intelligent difference in the community. It may sound strange but hardly anything promotes a greater sense of community than publishing diverse views on important local issues. Readers do not hold it against someone who writes a civil, reasonable letter opposing their views. These opinions show the community is vibrant and attempting to improve itself. Dialogue is the answer to most public problems.

The threat of libel hangs over every newspaper in the country, large or small. Litigation not only diverts the paper's energies away from publishing but the cost of such cases averages about $125,000 each. Although the editorial page enjoys more legal protection today than in the past, the state of libel law is confusing and causes some papers to be very cautious.

The U.S. Supreme Court, starting with *The New York Times* v. *Sullivan* in 1964, ruled that even a false and defamatory statement cannot be the basis for a legal suit if the publisher acts without an intent to misrepresent. The court said that plaintiffs could recover damages only after proving that the media statement was made with "actual malice." Such malice was defined as knowledge of falsity or reckless disregard for whether a statement was false. In cases since 1964, the high court clarified some aspects regarding libel but confused the public on others. *Gertz* v. *Welch* of 1974 was a landmark decision. The court left it to the states to determine the appropriate level of fault that plaintiffs would be required to prove. Most states have adopted a standard of "negligence," but others say a plaintiff must show that the defendant acted with actual malice. Most courts now hold that the First Amendment confers on opinion a legal immunity from defamation. However, the courts offer little guidance on distinguishing fact from opinion. Most editorial and columnist opinion concerns public figures who, by virtue of their positions, are not protected from malicious comment. One of the most important purposes of the First Amendment is to promote a vigorous marketplace of ideas and views. That is also the responsibility of the editorial page editor and, indeed, his readers.

Ed Scripps does not believe that the editorial page is the most important in his papers. He says it's the front page. He stresses that the first duty of a paper is to inform. That is the precise function of the day's most important stories on the front page. The primary aim of the editorial page is not to inform but to offer readers reasonable guidance on public issues—and, at times, to move readers to act in behalf of certain causes. Ed is convinced that a paper inspires more confidence in its integrity by conveying accurate and full information than by editorial and opinion writing. That is not to say a newspaper may somehow avoid having an editorial conscience. It must. But its major thrust should be information that the community needs to function in daily life.

Ed looks for humor in his and other newspapers. He once wrote in one of his personal journals: "I have learned that men and women like to laugh better than they do to cry. In a newspaper, humor is surprisingly more acceptable than heroics. I've learned that even a jolly rascal is a more acceptable companion to the average human being than the long-faced, stupidly honest man.

"Most people will always take the shortcut to their goals. This means that men like small papers and large type even more than they like completeness and beauty of style. The traveler likes beautiful scenery. The reader who wants a brief item of news prefers it in an interesting and attractive array rather than in a dull form."

Ed says that, in his lifetime, nothing has topped the "Li'l Abner" comic strip for humor. He still reads—and prints—the old comics. His readership surveys show they continue to be highly popular but nothing beats "Dear Abby" or "Ann Landers" for readership attention. He views these columns as offshoots of "Letters to the Editor." Scripps has long hired his own local columnists to write about everything from love to health and family matters. He says: "I have always tried to personalize our papers."

But that is not his first rule of newspapering. It still is to spell everyone's name correctly.

Ed has one pet peeve: badly written obituaries. He says that one of the marks of a good paper is to print well-composed obits. The lives of most people in small towns generally go unheralded, yet their contributions are often as great—if not greater—than individuals in large cities. Ed insists that a good reporter should find something interesting and informative in everyone's life.

Ed disagrees with those who believe that the editorial side of newspapers has more idealism than business staffs. He observes:

"The business side is dedicated to the paper's survival. It knows the risks and costs of putting out a paper every day. The New York *Times* may cover the news better than any paper in the country but it wouldn't be the great newspaper that it is without a dedicated, professional advertising department. Frankly, a lot of people buy the *Times* because of its first-rate and extensive advertising. The paper may well survive that fierce New York newspaper war more because of its advertising strength than its editorial clout. I look on all editorial and business staffs as equals. One could not exist without the other."

Ed continues to be a strong critic of newspaper unions. He maintains that unions have killed many papers in metro areas. Nevertheless, he insists that large papers can survive unions if they negotiate contracts well. However, Ed does not believe that small weeklies and dailies are strong enough to outlast unions. The major reason is cost. With unions, he estimates that his newspapers' cost per page would be four times what it is today. That would drive some league papers to the wall. Ed says his opposition to unions is a matter of survival, plus the fact that he doesn't want his internal newspaper policies—such as his emphasis on objective reporting—to be harassed by anatagonistic reporters who feel they will be protected by the Newspaper Guild.

Ed returns again and again to the word *freedom* in describing his views and career. That commitment was put to a major test in 1982. The Gannett Company, the country's largest newspaper concern, announced plans to purchase KRON–TV in San Francisco from Chronicle Broadcasting Company for a record-breaking $100 million, plus KOCO–TV, a Gannett-owned station in Oklahoma City. The media giant already owned both the Oakland *Tribune* and Marin County *Independent-Journal*. Gannett said it would sell the *Tribune* to comply with Federal Communications Commission regulations regarding newspaper-broadcast cross-ownership. However, it planned to retain the *Independent-Journal*.

The Scripps League owned the Novato *Advance* in Marin County and the Petaluma *Argus-Courier* in neighboring Sonoma County.

Ed was upset at "the further monopolization of the San Francisco market" by Gannett. He protested to the FCC that its regulations required Gannett to divest itself of the *Independent-Journal* before it acquired KRON–TV. Ed also told the FCC that since *USA Today*, the company's new national newspaper, was distributed in the San Francisco media market, it also violated FCC cross-ownership rules. He threatened to go to court if the FCC approved the deal.

Other newspapers as well as radio and TV stations, which did nothing about Gannett's proposed purchase, delighted in the story of the little Scripps League taking on giant Gannett.

After a year of Ed nipping at Gannett's Achilles heel, the news conglomerate threw in the towel. The *Chronicle* called off the deal and Gannett agreed. Gannett then sold the Oakland *Tribune* to its publisher, Robert Maynard, for $22 million.

Ed said later: "Anyone can compete with us in towns where the league has newspapers. But not everyone can go up against a giant like Gannett which may monopolize a market. We need some Davids against the Goliaths if media markets are to be based on freedom."

Even in these modern times, the greatest battle of newspapers continues to be for freedom—not only for themselves but for the legitimate aspirations of people around the world.

Actual freedom of the press, radio and TV exists only in the United States and perhaps Canada, where no prior restraints on published or spoken ideas are permitted. Only about thirty other nations have generally free news media, although the former Soviet Union and other former communist nations are on the road to media freedom.

That's why Ed and others support the Inter-American Press Association, which marked its fiftieth anniversary in 1992 at Seville, Spain. The meeting took place there to celebrate the 500th anniversary of the historical juncture of Spain and the Western hemisphere.

Ed thinks a lot about young people these days. Perhaps his choice of contemplation reflects the fact that he will pass the torch of league leadership to his wife and a younger generation. He has long dwelt on the people who have come to work for the league over the years.

Ed says the biggest advantages to these journalists are to gain

Ed Scripps at an Inter-American Press Meeting. From right: Bill Blethen, member of a well known Seattle newspaper family, Ed, William Cowles of the Cowles newspapers in Spokane.

experience, be allowed greater freedom than colleagues on larger papers, and enjoy a better quality of life—less crime, lower cost of living, less traffic, overcrowdedness and stress. The biggest disadvantages are lower pay and a heavy workload.

The major concerns of league editors these days are (in order of importance): the economy and competition from those outside the community; the ever-constant desire for more staff and resources, such as more money, added equipment, more newspaper color, and additional news space; the day-to-day management, publisher and owner problems; and staff turnover.

Studies, such as the one at Colorado State University, show that most editors across the nation are married, male, white, and over age thirty-six. Twenty-six percent are female. More than ninety percent like their work.

In contrast, most reporters and other journalists are female (fifty-one percent) and under thirty with forty percent single. Only nineteen percent are married with children. About sixty-six percent have graduated from college. Some forty percent chose the profession because of the work involved, while twenty-six percent say they became journalists as a matter of personal growth.

The news business has changed enormously since Ed began nearly seven decades ago. The drunks and drifters are gone. But so too are the wonderful, madcap times when reporters lived *The Front Page* of Ben Hecht and Charles MacArthur. Pay is better and hours are shorter. Much of the adventure and discovery in reporting—and writing—has slipped with the passing of such greats as Richard Harding Davis, Ernest Hemingway, Damon Runyon, Ernie Pyle, Homer Bigart and Bob Considine.

As E.W. passed his torch, it will soon be time for Ed to hand down his. Ed has a competent wife, sons, seven grandchildren, excellent executives and a good staff. The League has a solid future. But what about the future of small-town newspapers in general? That is the ultimate question.

11

THE FUTURE

What is a newspaper? What should a newspaper be? Will current newspapers be replaced by new informational systems and technologies in the next decade or two?

Every newspaperman and woman in the country is asking these questions. Many have been inquiring for the past decade—some even longer.

The new technologies are formidable—a widely expanding number of computer data bases—from news to business and medicine—fax services, audiotex and videotex. Faxes could provide the names of the nearest stockbrokers, shoe-repair shops and sandblasters. A man could program his TV audiotex to provide him with state business news while he was shaving in the morning. Videotex could offer photos of homes for sale.

Do these services constitute newspapers? No, they are information systems.

Some experts say the newspaper of the future will publish in

Ed and Betty Scripps in Palm Beach on their 40th wedding anniversary.
(*Mort Kaye Studios*).

printed form on a computer printer or screen or be broadcast and seen on a TV screen. Wire services, newspapers and broadcast services would continue to be the nation's basic news gatherers. Their reports, constantly updated with new information, would be sent electronically to homes. A "reader" can order—"program" in computer language—the entire newspaper or choose only parts of it, such as national and business news or sports. A newspaper also will be a multi-information source. Under PERSONAL, the paper may list your appointments for the day as well as electronic messages sent you during the night. Indeed, it may even enumerate the latest names of a dating service. Some shoppers have suggested that it list comparable prices at nearby supermarkets. If a news item appears important or interesting, the "reader" may request not only a longer story but even more background from another data base. Data bases extend into the wild blue yonder—from medical information to the history of the Nile River. Depending on what the subscriber wishes, the newspaper of the future can be a traditional paper in shorter form or an entire informational service.

Some subscribers are excited about the possibility of receiving specialized news—health, science or automotive news—on a daily basis. These reports would be as detailed as the *Daily Racing Form*, only intellectually upgraded. Some bargain hunters are intrigued with receiving a daily listing of nearby sales—even by item, such as spring suits or fall raincoats.

Ed Scripps is impressed with most technological advances and agrees these changes will dramatically affect the newspaper of the future. Yet he still asks a basic question: What is the function of a newspaper? Is it merely a conveyor of information or is the paper a forum where community information is exchanged, analyzed and argued. He believes that information is only one element in the makeup and life of a community. A newspaper is a catalyst that helps identify and formulate local concerns while citizens debate their merits and come to decisions about them.

Newspaper stories perform a valuable function in conveying information but these are only part of the paper's most significant contribution—the process of creating public policy and other ideas to build a better community. A paper must not only report but inform. Its purpose is not merely to print information but help develop opinion and serve the needs of a community—from supporting the police in fighting crime to helping raise money for a new community senior citizens center.

Ed feels that, if the most technologically advanced newspaper of the future does not identify with its readers and the community, it will become meaningless. At best, it will reflect a fact or a sound-bite. If it does not cover births, marriages and deaths well—and put them in the perspective of community development and progress— it will die in aimless mountains of data. The paper of the future must bring meaning to its readers' lives or it will have no social relevance. In a word, future newspapers must *care*.

Newspapers are like people. They fail not so much because of ignorance but indifference—or arrogance. Multi-information systems run the risk of intellectual distance and arrogance in a community setting. Those who propose their interconnection with computer and TV newspapers may actually be a threat to these future papers. These systems and, therefore, newspapers would be costly and not particularly accessible to many people.

Some news organizations have already learned this lesson. They experimented with news services on TV and computer screens in the 1970s and 1980s—and failed. These services were neither reasonably priced nor especially accessible. In particular, heralded videotex systems that would deliver on-line news to computer printers and become the new successors to papers sank in a sea of red ink. Today's conventional newspaper may have a much longer life than many experts think.

What are today's community editors and publishers saying about the future? What are their plans? Scripps League executives are no different from those on other small-town papers. This is what they say:

Roger Warkins, executive vice president: "Those who experimented with TV and computer news services weren't the only ones who went bust. So did some newspapers which went through the transition of computerizing their editorial and advertising work as

well as composing and press rooms. It became a mess. We set up
our own system and called it Scrippsat (Scripps satellite). We now
have a staff at our Herndon, Virginia, office that does nothing but
work to support each of our installations around the country.
We're constantly updating our computer systems. The Herndon
staff is on call seven days a week. The point is that we are keeping
up with technology but not taking leaps until they are reasonably
proven."

Rich Heintz, publisher of the Napa *Register*: "Readers expect
more today. Some small-town papers are becoming as sophisticated
as metropolitan dailies. The big papers are becoming direct competitors of small dailies. They're coming into our towns with informational services, phone ads, and direct mail. They can put out a
free shopper and hire a carrier service for total market coverage.

Barry Scripps's wedding to Gail De Vane, 1988 at La Jolla. From left: Blake
Scripps, Shayne Scripps, Barry, Gail, Kelly Scripps, Ed, Betty, Joanna
Scripps, Jim, Ed III and Bonnie Scripps.

The one thing that they can't do is cover our area as well as we do. We do a very good job of news coverage. That is how the small paper will survive—top news coverage.

"*USA Today* is a formula newspaper. We call it McNewspaper because it's like McDonald's formula food. It's bite-sized, quick and cutesy. I think there are still many people who want to learn about serious issues. We still do the in-depth story."

Bill Haigwood, publisher of the Novato *Advance*: "I know of no community newspaper publisher who has not lost a regional or national account in the recession-plagued economy of the past three years. Some of these accounts used to provide the base for our business and many of us took them for granted. Small retailers now make up the bulk of ad revenues for small papers. We're watching ad counts climb higher and higher while earnings remain static or decline.

"We have limited resources in the battle with big papers. One way of fighting back is to join forces with them to offer joint advertising programs. I've had experience with this and it has been very successful. We've held accounts that we otherwise might have lost. Fighting back may not be the whole answer. We might be better off redefining our niche and refocusing our attention on things metro papers cannot do. Just as the metros have squeezed themselves between the once-giant urban dailies and small community weeklies, we may need to face the music and create market share from business we never bothered about during the halcyon days of big grocery store ads. These are a few things that I'm currently doing:

"1. Developing a Newspaper-in-Education program for our local schools. They involve thirty classrooms in a nontextbook curriculum with cross-disciplinary applications (how education and newspapers interact). The program was developed for local papers by a teacher in our region. She amplifies it with workshops and instructional materials for a very reasonable annual fee. We expect to distribute up to 900 newspapers into the classrooms each week. The spinoff potentials are too numerous to mention.

"2. I favor Audiotex or an ads-on-call service to increase our classified advertising and give us an opportunity to sell 'info lines' to local advertisers who need to reach only Novato and want to pay an affordable rate for the service. The entire package is available to us for only $3,500. We can involve butchers, barbers, florists, et cetera, in affordable audio-text programs. Ten years ago, we might have given barbers and butchers an occasional call. Today, I can offer these people combined display/audio-text programs that are affordable and effective. There are a lot of advertisers out there who will advertise in the only affordable medium available to them.

"3. We've created a Welcome Wagon for newly arriving residents. Our community loses nearly one-quarter of its residents over each five-year period. We are losing loyal subscribers who are the basis of our circulation. To tap these newcomers, we offer them a New-comers Survival Kit. This offers them a Users Guide, phone directory, as well as coupons and premiums from advertisers (whom we charge a fee). About twenty-five percent of those who receive the kit take subscriptions to our paper.

"We pride ourselves on creating a public forum regarding local issues. We regularly run two full pages of readers' letters on every conceivable subject. Helping to shape a community's identity is key to any community newspaper's success."

John Shields, editor and publisher of the Santa Maria *Times*: "We're no longer just newspaper publishers. We're publishers. We're now printing a publication for realtors once a month. And we're now delivering it with our paper. We can print other publications. We're also involved with various information and advertising services. Competition in the communications field today is very keen. We have to make the most of our staffs, equipment and plant."

Kirk Parkinson, publisher of the Provo *Daily Herald*: "There is great economic pressure for small-town papers to move into job printing and audio-tech. With more people and equipment, we could also put out specialty publications: entertainment, family, health, youth, and real estate supplements. Our future is leading in these directions."

Jack Morgan, regional vice president: "We need to be more service-oriented but in a specific sense—making our papers more significant in the lives of their readers. Readers have got to know what is going on around them. We do not do as good a job as we must in educating the people in many aspects of daily life.

"Big papers are already moving into small towns. They team up with Ma Bell and sell more and more informational and advertising services that compete for the advertising dollar. They try to neutralize you on your own territory. Small-town newspapers must analyze where we fit. We can't be too many things to too many people. For one thing, we don't have the financial resources. Our strength is covering the local community.

"However, there are some relatively inexpensive ways for us to compete with large papers in these informational services and other devices. We've started at our paper in Petaluma, California, ads-on-call which places classified ads any time of the day or night. We can combine these with additional ads in the paper. We can target customers. We can do voice mail, direct mail or alternate delivery. In alternate delivery, we could deliver magazines instead of the postal service. We can do all these things and we eventually will. But we can't lose sight of the First Amendment. The basic difference between a newspaper and all these added services is that papers must keep people informed on what they need to know. The rest is interesting information."

Keith Curtis, research manager for the Scripps League: "Mr. Scripps is a philosophical man. For him, philosophy is a broad definition of research. In the 1960s, he began our research by interviewing readers and getting feedback from our papers. That was a lot more primitive than surveys are today. In the past ten years, the personal computer has made our benchmark surveys—performed every three to five years—very easy to do. They quickly tell us reader perceptions of each newspaper, household penetration, frequency of reading, and how much people are reading the competition. When we do a survey, for example in Provo, we return to surveys performed in the 1970s and compare them with today.

"I meet with the publisher and other news executives before a survey. We decide what we need to know. We make our contacts by telemarketing or a phone bank of trained callers who work nights and on weekends at the paper being surveyed. We find that using local people on site is best. We get as heavy a sample of opinions as we can. Sample questions are:

"What are you reading? When are you reading it? Do you believe the newspaper has gotten better? Worse? Why do you feel that way?

"As a result, we are now talking and thinking about our readership more than ever before. Basically, do they want to read the same news that is published in the paper each day? We've found out in our own and other surveys that readers often want much different coverage or stories than those chosen by editors. So we need to know what our readers are thinking. We have to balance local, national and international news in such a way that no reader will feel he will switch to a big-city paper.

"Mr. and Mrs. Scripps know the balance that they are looking for and I make regular reports to them. I know of no small newspapers which perform as much survey work as we do. It's a full-time job for me. One of the things we've learned in recent years affects advertising. We're trying to work with the telephone Yellow Pages in cooperative advertising. We work with wholesalers for them and don't reduplicate staff and paper work. We're also working with cable companies. We're now doing a lot of research in audio-text. Yet the league papers have a lot of independence and no two are the same."

Gregory Stevens, chief marketing officer: "More than a decade ago, some of the realities under which community newspapers had operated for decades began to change.

"Some formerly isolated markets were swallowed by expanding nearby metro areas and became suburbs. Peoples' lives were hooked elsewhere. The 'local news that you can't get anywhere else' became less important to some commuters.

"National advertising began to abandon smaller newspapers and

Ed with grandson
James G. Scripps on
the now-banned mo-
torcycle at Eagle Hill.

turn first to TV to reach America's grassroots, and then convert those former ad dollars to 'co-op' and promotion budgets.

"Chain retailers went to the suburbs and rural America. Downtowns began to dry up. One big store would replace ten to twenty mom-and-pops. That big store became more likely to preprint their own section for insertion in the paper—if they did not choose the mail—rather than running display ads in the paper. So community newspapers' page counts went down and newshole (space for news) shrank.

"Postal rates were reduced for bulk mailers, creating a wave of new mailed shoppers which competed for local retail ad dollars, classified lineage, etc.

"Recently, desktop publishing has allowed just about anyone with a computer and software to launch a neighborhood paper. These products nibble at the underbelly of community newspapers, even as some metro papers are looking at nearby community newspaper markets as good places to invent zoned (their neighborhood) editions.

"Faced with changes that reduce income, the natural—and often correct—reaction (of community papers) is to cut expenses somewhere. And/or raise prices so your remaining customers make up the dollars that you just lost. As an industry, that is what we did. To achieve short-term profit objectives, even the best of newspapers did both. Sometimes year after year. Over time this had a debilitating effect.

"After a while, some publishers found themselves with less experienced, less qualified staff; products with half the newshole (and therefore half the news value) that they'd had a decade ago; paid circulation that was hard to keep from continually slipping away (reflective of the less-valuable product) and competitors from above and below (invited into the market as the community newspaper weakened) wanting a piece of the newspaper's advertising pie, willing and able to undercut their ad rates."

Stevens points out that since the 1980s the Scripps League has

Ed with granddaughter
Joanna Scripps.

had to close several small papers that fell into a downward spiral. The league does not want to close any more and is taking protective action so that it won't have to do so.

The Santa Maria *Times* became a lab for product positioning. The newspaper made targeted investments in content, staff training, color, and job printing. All the while, it kept certain costs, those that would not hinder the paper's ability to move forward, at a minimum. The *Times* has advanced.

To further strengthen the league's papers, Ed and Betty Scripps created the post of research manager. This office is on call to offer market research so publishers can make more intelligent positioning decisions. Very few community papers have their own researcher on call.

In late 1991, the couple also created the position of vice president of marketing. Stevens has outlined a new program of plans and goals for the papers. These include proposed new profit centers, ranging from new publications to audio-text applications, and special projects that represent other new ideas.

Meantime, Ed Scripps keeps preaching that his newspapers must identify with their communities. He says: "That is the principal difference between us and Scripps-Howard."

He still fires off memos and ideas to his publishers and other executives:

—"Right now, newspaper stocks are down. But remember what the old farmer said: There are seven good years and seven bad years. That is the way life is."

—"It's now more difficult than ever to find good writers. Make the effort."

—"I see more newspaper mergers, including small papers. However, the merger of two competing newspapers does not mean the new organization will make a profit. For example, I don't think a merger of the *News* and *Post* in New York would necessarily mean a profitable paper. It might well create a paper on the margin that would make a pitiful return on investment."

—"If you are going to buy a newspaper, study its circulation receipts. The best buys among completely owned papers are those having the highest ratio of circulation receipts in proportion to the sale price. That may seem to be unusual mathematics but I believe it's absolutely true. The advertiser is attracted to circulation. Business begets business. In saying that, perhaps I am giving away a trade secret."

—"TV is a lazy process. Newspapers make readers think, discern, judge. Our papers do better where we have TV competition."

—"I think it's perilous to get into the cable TV business. It's not like making a permanent investment. The Federal Communications Commission is sometimes fair but not so in other instances. There's a lot of private politics involved. The FCC can change its controls and rules in rather short order. Suddenly your operation is paralyzed. It has lost much of its value through no fault of your own. I am attracted to businesses where the government can least interfere with them."

—"I am interested in the technological revolution now going on among newspapers, but I don't think that a lot of it will penetrate small papers. It would not be mathematically logical or cost effective in many instances. In the final analysis, it's the news that you print which makes or breaks a small paper—not frills. There is no substitute for in-depth reporting and local profiles. Computer graphics won't mean anything unless the paper has performed its basic reporting. We also must transform information into understanding."

—"I have nothing against desktop publishing. That is, using microcomputers to perform layout on screen and creating graphics. With a laser printer, it can deliver good-quality phototypesetting without chemicals. It is also a great timesaver. Young people with new ideas can start a paper with a few thousand dollars and leased equipment. But the question remains: Is the desktop newspaper delivering a responsible and in-depth news product? This business still demands a professional product."

—"The reason that smaller markets command a much higher percentage of gross revenues in the newspaper business today is the relocation of distributing centers—shopping malls and supermarkets."

—"One of the greatest challenges in newspapering today is to reach people who do not read or speak English."

—"I practice local autonomy to the maximum. I recognize the creative ability of our editors and publishers and allow them virtually complete freedom. There is no central control of news or editorial policy. My objective is to exchange ideas and information on all subjects, at all levels, and among all our papers. Control saps the dynamic quality necessary for growth. I have a very individualistic attitude toward journalism."

—"I am worried about the fact that we are becoming loaded with 'stars' in the newspaper, magazine and television news business. George Will, Pat Buchanan, Dave Barry and others are now celebrities as well as newsmen. Buchanan even became a presidential candidate, partly on name I.D. as a newspaper columnist and TV commentator. I am much more concerned about the long term of my papers than the short careers of individual men like Will, Buchanan and Barry. The business chews them up and eventually spits them out. We run columnists but my goal for our papers is long-term permanence. Our important mission is a legacy of community involvement and service."

—"My aim is to print the news. If an advertiser gets mad, so be it. If we are a good paper, if we maintain our circulation, that advertiser will return because he is primarily motivated by profit and his own survival. As far as I know, Sam Walton never got into this pettiness. He was simply interested in effective advertising. Business and newspapers are coworkers."

—"I still get a thrill out of walking into one of our papers and watching people covering stories, editing, selling ads and printing. A newsroom stimulates me like no other place in the world. It's so alive, sometimes even electric. Newspapering is such an interesting life. I love it."

The future of the league is entirely in Ed Scripps's hands. He made that clear in long meetings. Since he is now eighty-four years old, this raises three major questions: Does he have any plans to sell the league? If it continues, will it expand—and how? Who will succeed him as president?

Betty with her mother Eleanore Maynard Knight at the La Coquille Club luncheon at Palm Beach on Mrs. Knight's 93rd birthday.

Ed has no plans to sell the league. He and Betty were recently offered "a very substantial sum" to sell the papers but they turned it down.

"The league is not for sale," Ed declared. "There is a lot of future in it."

Since the league is privately owned and has no debt, he has no fear of a leveraged buyout attempt.

As long as Ed lives, he will be in the market to buy other newspapers. He believes that small papers have a bright future. However, he has no plans to buy into regular TV or cable operations because of the possibility of government interference and other uncontrollable risks. This includes the fear of losing some of his independence. Ed said:

"I keep sufficient cash on hand so that, if a good newspaper comes up for sale at a reasonable price, I am ready to buy. I don't

like to deal through brokers, rather with an owner directly. Today, if
you tell most owners that you will buy their paper for cash, they are
much more apt to make a quick deal. Most people want the money
here and now."

His wife Betty will, in all probability, succeed Ed. He puts it this
way:

"The league, the inheritance of our children and grandchildren
will best be preserved by the moral values inherent in her life. My
wife has a spiritual quality that dominates her thinking. She can be

Ed and John H. Perry, Jr., his longtime friend whose father represented
Ed's family. Two generations of friendship.

a taskmaster but she doesn't think only of the bottom line. She doesn't look at authority for power's sake. She is experienced, intelligent and, above all, honest."

League executives privately indicate that Ed has some reservations about his sons' executive abilities. However, he has exhibited no such doubts publicly.

"I am an old-fashioned man. A person should be known by his or her works. In other words, I believe in the survival of the fittest. Let them prove themselves. As I prefer to phrase it, let them surpass themselves.

"The important thing is for me to leave the organization strong. I don't think it's possible for me to command far into the future. Nature has a way of taking care of things. The strong survive."

Ed and Betty have made one final commitment to each other. They will be buried together in a place yet to be chosen.

Now, in the twilight of his career, Ed still talks of his father, mother and grandfather. He wishes that they had never fought and split. That is his bitterest memory and he will carry it to his grave.

Despite his long attention to profit, Ed has never been a man driven by money. He has often lamented the importance that others have attached to it. He says:

"In the end for a newspaper person, the thing that counts is whether your newspapers and your life have a soul. My grandfather was right. Soul—personal integrity—is the ultimate answer. Soul represents an individual's triumph over life."

INDEX